From Hurting to Healing

An Anthology

Revised Edition

Noire Publishing House

DEDICATION

To the hurting hearts in hiding, may you experience the beauty of healing by vulnerably living your truth and repurposing your pain to make life beautiful for God's children.

CONTENTS

ACKNOWLEDGMENTS

Candice "Ordered Steps" Johnson, thanks for working tirelessly and diligently to assist with the editing process. Your dedication and commitment are greatly appreciated. I look forward to our continued work together. You're truly blessed to be a blessing!

Lorna, thanks for recommending Candice's services and for making the connection. Also, thanks for the insight and resources you freely provided. Your contribution is truly appreciated–blessings in abundance.

Last but, not least, thanks to the extraordinary women on this project for their obedience to God. Each of you willingly answered the call to share your powerful testimony to impact lives, drawing on your strength, which lies in your ability to be vulnerable and authentic. Thank you for trusting me to lead and guide us in making life beautiful for others by helping them transition from hurting to healing. Words cannot express how blessed beyond measure I am to be on this journey with each of you. Our best is yet to come.

PREFACE

God gave me the vision for *From Hurting to Healing* at the start of this year. For weeks, I was awakened from my sleep during the early hours of the morning. Like clockwork, between 3 a.m.-4 a.m., I would arise. I've heard that when God wakes you up at this time, He wants to get your attention. He either wants to talk to you and download something in your spirit, or He wants to hear from you and listen to your prayers and petitions.

I had just wrapped up a three-month-long season of praying daily at midnight with my co-author Simone and her friends. We met faithfully five days a week to wage war against Satan and his demons, combating the attack they relentlessly unleashed on us and our loved ones. My eyes were wide open to the tricks and tactics of the enemy. I was tired of Satan wreaking havoc in my life and in the lives of those I loved. The prayer warrior in me was reawakened and ready for battle!

Each morning I'd spring out of bed and obediently assumed my position of surrender, kneeling in prayer by my bedside. I'd pray fervently for my loved ones and myself. Some mornings I'd read the Word and then sit in silence waiting for God to speak to me. Other mornings, I'd pace my living room floor and converse with God or sing worship songs from the depths of my heart. I also journaled to express my innermost thoughts and release it all to God. But, as time went on and sleep deprivation kicked in,

I became less enthusiastic about my early morning sessions with God.

One morning, I flat out asked Him what He wanted. "I'm praying, talking to you, reading the Word, and praising you," I frustratedly said. "What do you want from me?" "I just want to sleep!" I was so mad I said a quick prayer from the comfort of my bed and rolled back over to go to sleep. But sleep evaded me because God wasn't done. Finally, He spoke, "Hurting to Healing," I heard Him say. In that moment, I figured He was downloading the title for my next book. It made sense because I was in the midst of a dark season, healing from a broken heart. I jotted the title down in my journal and went back to sleep.

But something didn't sit well in my spirit about my conclusion. Over the next few days and weeks, I tried to make sense of it. At the time, I actively participated in a large Christian group on Clubhouse. In fact, I frequented several faith-based groups on Clubhouse. While each group had its own purpose, style, and dynamics, the one commonality was the hurt and pain expressed by God's children. My heart shattered as I listened to men and women vulnerably talk about failed marriages/relationships, sexual assault, abuse, addiction, mental health challenges, suicidal ideation, etc. Wanting to help, I approached the moderator of the large Christian group and offered to facilitate free writing workshops to help people release their pain and begin the healing process through journaling. But God foiled my plan because His plans are always greater than ours.

As I was showering one day, God spoke to me clearly, informing me that *From Hurting to Healing* would be an anthology with myself and twenty other women. My first response was to laugh because God is funny and has jokes. "I don't even know 20 women", I retorted. He immediately began downloading the names of people in my spirit who would be a part of this project. Many of whom were family members, friends, or acquaintances with powerful testimonies. Over the next few days, He also divinely connected me with beautiful souls I met on Clubhouse, who eagerly accepted my invitation to be a part of this project. I was in awe and amazed by their willingness, but in hindsight, these divine connections came as a result of our obedience. Without hesitation, I began working diligently on this purpose project with limited experience and resources.

Almost immediately, I came under spiritual attack because I was doing the will of God. By the end of the first Zoom meeting with my co-authors, I was bent over the toilet vomiting while Simone closed the meeting with a powerful prayer of petition. I was so weak and ill that I laid in bed the whole next day. In another instance, depression reared its ugly head one weekend, resulting in countless tears of frustration. Then there were the many stumbling blocks along the way that tried to deter me. But God reminded me of His faithfulness to bring **HIS VISION** to fruition. So, I forged ahead with the assignment. My co-authors and I banded together to pray and encourage, uplift, and support one another. Daily, I found renewed strength and energy from their testimonies and the growth/transformation I witnessed; I knew that I had to keep pushing for them, for us, and for the powerful messages we shared that others needed to hear. By the grace and mercy of God, we present to you *From Hurting to*

Healing: An Anthology–the beginning of a beautiful, life-changing journey for all.

Healing Across Borders

ADRIENNE MARTIAN

Culture is one of those things that like my skin tone, falls outside of my control and wasn't something I got to choose. Don't get me wrong, I am a proud first-generation Guyanese and Haitian-American. But despite my immense love for my heritage, the feeling wasn't always mutual. Growing up, I felt different, like I failed the test. I wasn't quite Guyanese or Haitian enough, and definitely not American enough, either. Being stuck between worlds is the best way to describe it. For as long as I can remember, I've sought to connect those worlds and belong.

One of my earliest memories was an evening in Guyana around the age of four or five. It was dinner time, and the familiar symphony of insects serenaded me from outside. My grandparents were very traditional and would sit at the dining table for nearly all of our meals. My grandmother made sure the dining table was aesthetically pleasing with lace doilies, glass candle holders, and my grandfather's homemade pepper sauce amongst other things. Needless to say, this was a central place in our home where memories were imprinted on our souls. This particular night was no exception.

Looking back, I still feel a twinge of sadness because of the narrative I created surrounding this moment. I was standing between the dining and living room, overjoyed by a childish epiphany, giddy with excitement. I don't actually remember the events that preceded my profound announcement, probably because I was so preoccupied with my thoughts. But standing there, I remember having the biggest smile on my face as I turned to my grandmother and called her "Mom!"

I'm sure you were expecting something far more dramatic; however, that life-changing moment was the first time I'd ever called anyone mom. When I said it, either out of pity or kindness, no one corrected me. See, I felt like I'd found something I didn't even know I'd been missing in my life: a mother figure. This is probably my earliest memory of actively seeking a parental connection and craving a sense of belonging.

It's probably worth explaining how I got to that point. By the grace of God, I'm not an orphan, and my mother is still with me as I write this at the age of 32. My genesis starts with my birth in Brooklyn, where I lived with my parents until the age of three. Based on the stories my mother has shared over the years, my grandmother came up from Guyana to help my parents raise me. Their lives were so busy; they simply didn't get to spend much time with me. My mother always rushed to get me to daycare so she could get to work on time, then hustled to pick me up and get dinner ready, and so on. Being the gracious woman my grandmother was, she offered to take me to Guyana to raise me.

I lived with my grandparents in Georgetown until I was six. I have many fond memories of the time I spent there walking on the sea wall, picking mangoes and cherries in the backyard, and playing with my friends at St. Agnes Primary School. My emotional and cultural identity was forged there.

I don't remember the exact day I was told it was time for me to return to the U.S., but I do remember living in our one-bedroom apartment in Jamaica Estates. To a six-year-old who'd spent half of her life in a "third-world" country, the single bedroom apartment felt lavish. By no means was my family in Guyana destitute, but the infrastructure there is different. For one, blackouts were common, and if you're not familiar with the smell of kerosene, it's probably because you haven't had to light a lantern to find your way through the house without power. Life in the states took some getting used to; the jury is still out on whether life here is "better," so I'll just stick with "different" for now.

Growing up in Queens, most of my family stateside were Haitian (my father's side). For me, this was a bit of a culture shock to say the least: the food, language, mannerisms, and music. Being sheltered by my grandmother, the highlight of my television viewing experience included *Matlock*, *Three's Company*, maybe *Knight Rider* if no one was looking. So, things like *Snick*, *WWE*, and entertainers like Mase and Foxy Brown were a whole new world to me. To make things worse, I had a thick accent that my cousins teased me about. "I can't understand what you're saying," they told me. Trust and believe, it didn't take long for me to lose my accent, and I haven't looked for it since.

Adjusting to the culture got easier with time, but I still get tested. Whether it's the need to explain why I don't speak Creole (because my mother is Guyanese and I grew up in Guyana), or when someone says something in Creole, then asks me to translate what they said. Invariably, the exchange ends with them chuckling as I struggle to decipher context clues. Often, I risk losing my "Black card" because I've never watched *A Different World* or can't recite the lyrics to a song by TLC. I would like to say that need to prove I am FILL IN THE BLANK enough goes away (the blank could be any one of my cultures), but the honest truth is, that feeling doesn't go away–I simply choose not to give it the power I once did.

In retrospect, attending a welcome home party thrown by your parents whom you don't really know or remember could easily sound like a script from *This Is Us*. In my 6-year-old mind, I was just swept up in the excitement of being somewhere new. Moving from adolescence to young adulthood, I realized certain bonds and connections just weren't there for me. Even into my late twenties, I was plagued with questions about why my parents gave me away and chose not to raise me.

I'm not guided by astrology; however, I've realized I'm an emotional Pisces, and the feisty Aquarian, otherwise known as my father, were like oil and water. If I ever asked questions that had the potential to make my father feel a certain way, I was doused in a tsunami of rage and deprecation. I jumped into defense mode to weather the storm, and in the end, I was physically unscathed but

4

emotionally beaten. I was left with no answers and felt disconnected and lost. I was hurt because I truly wanted to connect with my parents, but daring to unearth their truth left me seeking isolation. It wasn't until I created bonds with others outside my family or made friends with other Haitians that I realized the cycle of anger, verbal abuse, and isolation I was enduring wasn't normal.

Going through this cycle ironically had the fortunate and unfortunate effect of building my resilience. The negativity made me tougher and stronger; I heard all the worst things about myself at home, so facing the world was never an issue. Unfortunately, this also made it harder for me to connect with others, trust them, or seek support. I taught myself to isolate, fend for myself, and find my own answers, which created multiple layers that took years to unravel and reprogram.

Ultimately, it took surrounding myself with positive people who held me in high regard and weren't afraid to offer praise or encouragement for me to realize I am a kind, generous, and worthy woman. I had to reprogram the way I thought of myself, the way I saw myself in the mirror, and the way I spoke about myself. I had to stop believing what my father said about me and start listening to the truth I knew about myself. I realized I didn't need to forgive my mother for forcing me to be my own savior; in actuality, I probably need to thank her.

Subconsciously I was envious of other kids who grew up with parents that raised them to identify with their culture and taught them their native language. I wanted my parents to be the Winslows from *Family Matters*. I tried to cast my parents into the role I created for them. When they didn't show up the way I scripted them, I checked out and constructed a world where my friends were my family. The truth of my teens and young adult life is that I was stuck in my childhood, in my grandparent's dining room where I crowned my grandmother "Mom." To heal from feeling abandoned and disconnected from my parents, I had to stop judging my experience and labeling it as "less than" the other kids.

Once I was able to rewrite my narrative from abandoned to loved, I saw my parents for who they are and have accepted them, flaws and all. It's a daily choice that starts with choosing to be kind to myself first. As a parent recovering from abandonment issues, I have moments where I push myself beyond my limits; however, I recognize those instances are rooted in a narrative which simply wasn't true. Abandoned was the lie I told myself to keep feeling victimized as opposed to empowered and worldly. The empowered me strives to parent from a place of balance and self-love, so I can pour into my girls and teach them to be emotionally and culturally evolved.

Time is the most precious gift that God gives us. As part of my continued healing, I am focused on the time I have here on Earth to spend with my loved ones. Every day I choose to spend more time with my family, being present in the moment as opposed to living in reaction to the past. I intentionally create opportunities for my daughters to bond with their grandparents and learn about their culture while also creating safe spaces for them to express their individuality.

No Turning Back

ANDREA MOSES

May 19, 2020, is a day I will never forget. Why? Because the week before, I was drowning in addiction and depression and had reached the point that I was slowly killing myself. It needed to stop. The pain, the hurt–it had to end. Drinking, drugging, and depression catapulted me to a very dark place; something had to be done.

Desperate for help but too scared to take the first step to get it, I called a facility and hung up after the first couple rings out of shame and fear. I couldn't believe I was actually admitting I had a problem. I told a friend I'd cheated myself out of the first step, and she encouraged me not to give up. So, I called the facility again. A sweet lady answered the phone, and I asked if they had any beds available. After asking me a round of preliminary questions about my history, she instructed me to call back in a few days to check the status of my application. I was so relieved not to have to start treatment that day.

I called back on May 18th and was told to come in the next day to begin the process. I was instructed to bring a few of my personal belongings in case I was admitted. Suddenly, reality hit me in the face like a truck, and I didn't know how to handle it. I reached out to my support system and informed them how I was changing my life. Everyone was supportive of me which helped, but didn't relieve my anxiety. Still, I sucked it up and packed a bag of necessities for my possible stay. Afterward, I went straight to my bottle and stash of drugs to take the edge off things. This would be my last time putting harmful chemicals in my body.

The day I reported to the facility, I hopped in my friend's car, not knowing what to expect. Thank goodness I was exhausted from all the partying I'd done the night before. I was so out of it; I couldn't even talk myself out of what I was about to do. Once we got there, I walked in and was told to take a seat. After what seemed like forever, my name was finally called; I had officially checked into rehab. I couldn't believe that I was actually doing this.

The admission process was excruciating. By the time they finished, my body had begun detoxing. I was asked all sorts of questions about my addiction, which were so intrusive, I was ready to get it over with. To make matters worse, I still hadn't been advised whether a bed was available for me or not, which drove me nuts. It felt like an eternity, but I was finally told to bring in my luggage because I was being transferred to the facility where I would be housed.

I walked outside to gather my things from the car and was greeted warmly by an escort. She was extremely sweet to me and gave me a glimpse of hope because she was in recovery as well. By looking at her, no one would've thought she'd been an addict, too. With a heavy sigh, I retrieved my luggage from the car and told my friend goodbye. I strolled back inside and waited until a cab came to take me to the next location. As I waited, I wondered if anyone could tell I had binged the night before. My body was worn down from lack of rest, so I was eager to just lay down anywhere. Luckily, the cab showed up quickly, and I hopped in. On the ride to the facility, I was both eager and frightened to start recovery. Once inside, I had to go through another intake process, but a kind staffer met me and assured me that God sent me there. I will never forget her kind, prophetic words.

Once the paperwork was completed, I was happy to get my room assignment because I'd finally be able to lay down. When my head hit the pillow, I closed my eyes for some much-needed rest. When I woke up the next day and didn't know where I was, reality hit me. I was really in rehab, getting treatment for my addiction. There was no turning back at this point. I showered, put on a cute black and white dress, and went outside in search of food. There were women everywhere who all gawked at me like the new girl on campus. Eventually, several of them came over and introduced themselves. They informed me about the do's and don'ts of the facility. I was somewhat freaked out that I didn't have access to my cell phone or cigarettes. How would I survive without them? I quickly reasoned that was the least of my worries; I had to make the decision to be all in so I could get through this.

I made a conscious decision to put in the work that would change my life. It was going to be hard, but I had to create a better life for myself. I was afraid of the unknown, but I refused to give up. I put God as the head of my life on my road to sobriety. Healing meant working through those things I carried around for years. It required vulnerability. I didn't like talking about my feelings or problems, but in order for this to work, I had to open my mouth and speak my truth.

I attended group sessions every day, which helped me learn how to be open and share my feelings. It took a lot of effort, especially after sitting in the back of class, listening to others share their trauma. I didn't think I'd ever be bold enough to share my troubles in front of people who knew nothing about me. But one day, I broke down for the first time in a group session. This particular group was more intimate; there were fewer people, which helped my comfort level.

That was the first time I allowed myself to feel such emotion in years. See, I was an expert at suppressing my feelings. I numbed my pain for over a decade, but that day I released so much pain, it freaked me out. Thinking I was too tough to cry, I tried gathering myself so that I wouldn't sob like a baby in front of everyone; however, I allowed myself to go with the flow. Working through every emotion that had been tucked away, I was finally free of the pain I'd been carrying around for years.

I'm so proud of myself for finally discussing my feelings openly. From that day forward, I wanted to share more often, but it wasn't easy. I'm an introvert, so my anxiety flared up at times because talking in front of people scared the crap out of me. Every time I wanted to share my feelings in a large group setting, I somehow talked myself out of it. In fact, I ran in the other direction, telling myself I'd go through with it the next time. Then I began practicing what I'd say over and over in my head and found myself sharing more, just not in the way I wanted to. But I was happy I at least opened my mouth, and people listened to me. Recovery wasn't just for me to sober up, I was challenging myself.

I couldn't accomplish any of these things without the help of God. With daily prayer, things got easier. As I neared my ninety days at the facility, it was time to decide what was next for me. Initially, I wanted to go home until I realized I needed more than ninety days to heal from all the pain I endured. My counselor mentioned another facility to me, which I automatically declined in my head. I needed to talk to God first. He calmed my spirit, and I chose to continue uncovering my truth.

I proceeded to the next step in my recovery and healing process, and I'm glad I've made it this far. I still struggle with being completely transparent, but I've come a long way. During the process, I had a chance to shed a lot of things I needed to let go of. Although the work is a lifetime commitment, I am more at peace with choosing recovery.

There are so many positive things happening for me in this new phase. I reconnected with my support system and have a better relationship with God. I've also met so many amazing people on this journey. Recovery has truly changed my life for the better, and I love every bit of it. I've also discovered my purpose in life is to share my testimony and how God has brought me through. I want others to see that with God's help, they can turn their life around, too.

I want to continue encouraging and supporting those who've walked a similar path as me. Although every day, I fight to heal from the trauma of alcohol and drug use and mental illness, I know there's a way out for me as long as I keep God first and put in the work to stay on the right path. My powerful testimony will inspire others to stay the course because God is faithful and will bring them through. He did it for me and will do it for them too.

Thank God for all that I've learned during this journey. It has helped me become the woman that I am today. I am unapologetically me!

Guilt, Shame, and Fear

AZIZAH MCENTIRE

"Azizah? Azizah! How could you do this to me? Hello? Answer me!"

The sound of my heartbeat matched his voice. It was a deep, uncomfortable pounding that swelled in my neck, numbed my eardrums, and burned my insides. I was mute as I held the phone to my ear, so numb that my feet couldn't feel the brown wooden floors sustaining the heavy load I was carrying. Unable to sit down, I stood in silence. It would have been better for me to fall to my knees and land on the air mattress I'd slept on the previous night, but it was deflated and tucked away. I was desperate to let the air out of myself too, so that I could disappear into a state of non-existence.

He continued screaming in my ear as I froze in place, alone in my mother's apartment for the first time since moving back home two months prior. Mom was afraid to leave me by myself. If I stayed in the bathroom too long, she tapped on the door, her anxiety seeping through the wall as she waited for a response. In the two short months that I'd been there, I lost fifteen pounds along with any motivation to live through each day; however, on this particular morning before my husband called, I was pushing for a better day. I'd woken up rejuvenated, ready to move on with my life and put the past behind me. For so long, I believed moving on meant hiding what couldn't be undone, yet God had other plans. It's amazing how He'll intervene when we think we've found the answer but fail to be in alignment with His purpose for us.

For a while, I ignored God's signs because I didn't want to do what I was created to do; I wanted to do what I wanted to do. Consequently, I embarked on a merry-go-round of confusion until I lost my balance and my life spun out of control. Eventually, I was confronted by my poor decisions and was being forced to tell the truth. Confessing meant confronting the hurt I held onto for years, which meant pulling off layers of childhood trauma. I didn't want to do it, but I was taught a valuable lesson: secrets will keep us stuck, no matter how well we think we can hide them.

Gripping the phone, I held on even tighter to my lies. Truth was a language that hadn't existed between us for a long time. Although we were married, we were separated by more than 300 miles in distance and in heart. Between the loud chatter clouding my brain and the incessant thumping of my heart, I began to talk myself out of confessing. *Just pretend you don't know what he's talking about. He can't really know. How could he? YOU take control and ask him questions. Whatever he says, say it's a lie and ask for proof.* "What are you talking about?" I finally responded.

"Azizahhhhh!"

His gruff voice was so loud it crashed against my gut like a fist with every syllable of my name. I wanted him to hang up the phone, but he continued screaming my name as he waited for an answer. Suddenly, his screams sounded like a lone wolf howling for revenge after its tribe became the prey. I pictured his face with tears rolling down his cheeks; my mind raced as I listened to him grappling to breathe through his tears. *He doesn't know; he just heard rumors and is calling to see if you'll confess.* Prepared to hang up without a response, I heard him say, "Azizah, I know you were on the news. It's all over the internet." Those were his last words before he ended the call.

When I raced to search my name on the internet, my mugshot instantly appeared. The further I scrolled, I discovered several websites reporting my arrest. I collapsed to the floor and held my head in between my legs. Like Eve, I was naked in front of the world but without a companion to share the shame of eating the forbidden fruit. Hesitantly, I clicked on a website where the headline read, **Prison Bars Couldn't Stop Their Love, but an Arrest Might.** The comments were filled with insults. People who didn't know me were weighing in on a story they knew nothing about. Phone clutched in my hand, I laid on the floor and read every single comment. I was already dealing with my arrest, now the whole world knew. I was the new face of mockery and stupidity.

Sobbing uncontrollably, my weeping was interrupted by my ringing phone. "Mommy," I cried when I saw it was her on the line.

"What's wrong?" she asked.

"They know! Everybody knows what I did. He called me and said I was on the news!" I wailed between tears.

Mom fell silent. She was at the store with my youngest son, but before leaving, she asked if I was going to be okay. As unreasonable as it sounds, her question humiliated me. I was already at home following a failed marriage, scandalized at my job, and now I had my mother more concerned about my well-being than that of my two and five-year-old sons.

"So what if they know, he knows, or anyone else. So what, Azizah? Now you stop that crying," she reprimanded.

"But people are talking about me all over the internet and calling me names, Mommy. I feel so stupid."

"Azizah, you have to get yourself together and get your baby from school. Forget those people, they don't know you. And I wish he would call me and say anything after all that he's done!"

"Ok, Mommy."

After disconnecting the call, I forced myself to regroup. I went to the bathroom to wash my face, and when I looked in the mirror, I was reminded of the 9-year-old little girl who'd go into the bathroom, look in the mirror, and cry over what she saw. I hated my features. I critiqued and wished away every part of me. Now, as I peered at myself, I asked God why He made me at all. I considered breaking the glass and slitting my wrists, but I thought of my mother and the mess she'd be forced to clean if I did. I splashed more water on my face and rested my hands on the sink as I held my head down and allowed the moisture to drip off my face into the basin. My phone rang, but I ignored it. It rang again; still, I ignored it. When the house phone rang, I allowed the answering machine to pick up the call.

"Azizah, Azizah, pick up the phone," my mother's voice shouted.

I wanted to ignore her, but I hated hearing her panic. I rushed into the living room and picked up the phone. "Mom, I'm okay. I was in the bathroom; I'm getting dressed and leaving right now."

"Oh, okay," she said with a nervous laugh. "I was just checking to see if you needed anything from the store."

"No, I'm fine. Thank you," I said as I hung up.

I wasn't okay. I hadn't been for a while, but I didn't see the point in telling my mother the truth. I left the apartment and walked outside with tears rolling down my face. Hurt, hopeless, and ashamed, it felt like the world was judging me. When I walked outside, each time someone glanced in my direction, I wondered if they'd seen me on the news and commented online. As I continued walking, I spotted a big white truck barreling down the street towards me. I started convincing myself that when it got closer, I'd jump in its path. As my heart beat through my ears, drowning out the sounds in the busy Brooklyn streets, God intervened. He showed me an image of my body sprawled on the pavement, with my mother weeping over me. It hurt to imagine her in pain, even though I believed she'd be better off without me.

Next, an image of my son sitting on a wooden bench with his feet dangling as he swung them back and forth flashed in front of me. His face was drenched in sadness as he asked his teacher why his mommy hadn't come to pick him up yet. That image hurt me to the core; he'd never understand why I had to leave. The image of his grief was more painful than the misery I was in. I loved my children more than I thought I could ever love anyone. I didn't want my suicide to make them question my love for them or have a mugshot as the last image of their mother. My boys didn't deserve to be burdened with unanswered questions. That day, I found the strength I didn't know I had and let the truck pass me by.

Guilt, shame, and fear tore holes into my back as I reminisced on what got me to this dark place. When I was 31, I was arrested for having an affair with an inmate in a New York State prison. My job was to meet with incarcerated individuals and help with their rehabilitation back into society. I started off in the main counseling office, sharing a large office with 15 other people. After a while, I was moved to the transitional services office in a permanent space behind the prison gates that had a private office with a door I could freely open and close.

I facilitated transitional groups that every prisoner was required to attend whether entering the facility or about to be released. My job was to prepare both sets of prisoners for life inside and outside those walls. One of my responsibilities was facilitating a group conversation which I called "The PREA Talk." PREA stands for Prison Rape Elimination Act. My talks began like this, "If you are the victim of unwanted sexual contact between yourself and another prisoner, these are the steps you can take." Then I'd show a video in which formerly incarcerated men shared their experiences about sexual assaults behind bars. Most of the time, the group laughed at the video. As I tried to reiterate the seriousness of rape in prison, I added, "Sex with a state employee is also not allowed and can never be considered consensual. If you have any sexual contact with a prison employee, that employee will be arrested, and you will probably go to solitary confinement while the incident is investigated."

I knew the rules well because I recited them at least once a week, yet I broke them. I walked into that prison every day feeling broken. Still, I mustered up the strength each day to share messages of hope with my clients but returned home at night, feeling zero relief. My self-esteem was low, my husband was cheating, and I felt unseen and worthless. How did I get there? How would I break free from the imprisonment from my own mind? I held onto irrational beliefs and misplaced blame. All of the stories I clung to were reflective of the hurt I allowed to lead the way. I was so broken; I was desperate for anything to ease the pain. Following my arrest, I felt as though my unhealed pieces were bonded together.

How could I be so stupid?

We've all done it. Mentally beating ourselves down, which does nothing but make us feel even more beat the hell down. I was on the news, in the newspaper, and seven pages of internet search results. There wasn't a rock large enough for me to hide if I wanted to. Fear stopped my life dead in its tracks. I was afraid of going to prison, afraid I wouldn't get a new job, and afraid to walk down the street. I feared people would recognize me and would ridicule me. What I was fearful of the most was losing my children.

What I didn't know then was, if there is something strong enough to stop you, then there is also another force that is strong enough to put you back on track. It was up to me to choose which force I was going to follow. The truth is, sometimes it takes an earthquake or two to realign our world. I don't know what the earthquake moment is in your life, but if you're honest with yourself, you know. I'm not talking about the childhood memories which cause us pain; it's the incidents that arise because we're still holding onto our past. It's about the person in your life that you can't seem to let go of yet blame when your world crumbles. It's what made you pick up this book, what led us to "meet" spiritually.

Yes, that.

When our lives shift, sometimes we ask ourselves why or why me? I had all the reasons why I shouldn't have been on the news, and even more reasons why over 50,000 people shouldn't have been talking about me on social media outlets, or why I shouldn't have lost my job and been forced to take a walk of shame past my co-workers. I was so caught up; I couldn't see clearly and was on the wrong path for a long time. I was masking issues I couldn't hide anymore and was tired of falling repeatedly and getting up, only to fall deeper into the same hole. I just knew that I wanted a change, but I didn't know what that change consisted of.

Feeling alone, all of my whys resurfaced. The most painful why was, *Why isn't there anybody else like me?* I searched online for forums with people who experienced the same magnitude of guilt, shame, and fear that I had to relate to them so I wouldn't feel so alone. Unfortunately, I never found the right fit. If I'm honest, I didn't really want support–I wanted others to feel my pain, which was an unhealthy and unrealistic goal. No one can ever feel our pain. There may be similarities, but it's never exactly the same. I began to learn what I'd been counseling people on for years: the power of our minds. I had to gain clarity on what was best for me and understand my feelings. I wanted people to see how isolated I felt. Our stories don't have to be the same in order for there to be healthy support; my story might not be like yours, but you are not alone.

Despite negativity and self-loathing, there was a small nudge trying to pull me back on track. I had to choose to listen to that small but mighty force refusing to let my story end in despair. I fought to pull myself out of the rubble. You have that voice too; you just have to listen to it. Listen to your small, mighty force, so you can pull yourself up and conquer what once tried to bury you.

I learned to embrace every piece of me I believed was broken. I couldn't take anything I'd done back and didn't have the power to undo my mistakes. I fully embraced my arrest, my failed marriage, the childhood scars, and every mistake I made. In order to love myself, I had to love all of me. Once I got that revelation, my life completely changed. I activated change right where I was, in my childhood home, without waiting for things around me to start getting better first. Once I began working on myself, everything else fell into place. I made a decision to stop letting fear rule my world and stopped shrinking myself. I refused to accept less than I deserved as a way to fit in and took control of my situation. External changes weren't going to benefit me; I needed to move, not the mountain.

Every tragedy I endured brought me to sharing this story. I wasn't alone like I thought I was–there were people who were just like me who needed to know they weren't alone either. My actions and mistreatment from others was fueled by a lack of self-worth. At first, it was hard to admit I was struggling with low self-esteem because I viewed it as something to be embarrassed about. In my mind, lack of confidence is frowned on by society, and in my case, was an indication that something was wrong with me. It hurt even more when I tried to push my feelings aside and pretend they didn't exist. If I was going to heal, I needed to examine myself–starting with my current situation.

My transformation didn't happen overnight. It was a gradual and initially painful process, as life wasn't getting better for me. I was sinking deep and fast. I left one unhealthy relationship and started an illegal affair. In spite of my pain, I had to take an honest look at myself. I was settling for less than I deserved and felt undeserving of my own love. You deserve to be loved and cherished and respected. You also deserve for your happiness to be independent of others. I am sharing my story because I want you to know that the only person responsible for making you happy is you. The rest will follow.

I no longer hide from my past or doubt that I'm worthy. Through God's grace, I'm able to share my own story instead of someone sharing it as a memory in the event of my death. I'm not another statistic; I'm a testimony of what it looks like when you rise above adversity, forgive yourself, love yourself, and choose YOU.

Today, I am an entrepreneur, a homeowner, and in a loving, committed relationship. I own a private practice therapy business called *Healing On Us*. I counsel people every day and provide the tools they need to help them go from tragedy to triumph. My life didn't change because a magical door was opened; it changed because I fully opened the doors I tried to close. I faced my trauma, recommitted my relationship with God, loved myself, and made a decision not to turn back.

I thought my arrest was the worst thing that could happen to me, unaware that five years later, I would grow so much that my life would change in unexpected ways. T.D. Jakes said, "God isn't trying to change your mountain. He is using your mountain to change you."

Lord, I thank You for my mountain.

From Ending to Beginning

CAMYLLE HILL

The greatest gem that my father ever gave me was one that I didn't understand until I turned thirty-five: The decisions we make now affect our immediate future. It is a revelation that eluded me for two decades since the consequences of my choices had never caught up to me. I spent my youth (can I call zero to thirty years old, youth?) believing I was undefeatable, which wasn't too much of a stretch considering my choices never held me accountable.

When I reflect on my hero's journey, I'm grateful to realize that God has always and will always cover me. Even before high school, I moved mountains with an unshakable level of resilience I was completely oblivious to. It wasn't until college that my friends dropped the bomb that the childhood experiences I shared with them were far from normal. Not only did realizing I was an overcomer feed my faith, but it also, stealthily and steadily, *fed my ego*. I was untouchable.

By the time I left college--pregnant and confident, I knew that if I just followed where God led, if I allowed myself to write, reflect, love, and bring light to all things, He would not let me fail. And He didn't. **Before the end**, I found myself blessed with a career I adored, two wonderful children, a huge place in a beautiful, kid-friendly neighborhood with fantastic schools, and the type of friends you win at life with.

It's hard having everything you want, when you want more than you can handle. I found myself living on a super tight schedule, operating off less than two hours of sleep a night, driving to meetings in other cities then hustling home to shuttle the kids to their activities, volunteering in the community... running, running, running. It was the epitome of insanity. But it's what I wanted, right?

I traded devoting my attention, time, and care from being excellent at a few things for mediocrity in many areas of my life so I could have it all. I skated through the days making irresponsible and inconsiderate decisions--turning my world into a powder keg just waiting for the right stimuli to set off a massacre. I agreed to work on projects I didn't truly have time to complete in excellence, while ignoring my children's slipping grades and increasingly challenging behavior. I even tried bribing them into academic submission so I could focus on making money. But being reckless with my funds, I found it difficult to pay my bills despite the long hours I worked. I flaked on my friends and played with the emotions of any man who showed an interest in me. Worst of all, my actions depleted the time I once devoted to God. Disintegration was inevitable.

The beginning of the end started with a phone call at

midnight.

"Hello?"

"Your sister has been arrested."

I'm positive there was conversation following this revelation, but I can't recall what it was. "Blah, blah, blah," is all I heard, then, "Her sons are here at the police station." "Blah, blah, blah...your nearest sibling with available space is in the hospital...blah, blah, blah...are you able to accommodate them?"

My mouth said yes, but my heart and mind were in too much chaos to actually agree. If I had known that the lesson my father had been trying to teach me would show up all these years later, I would've made some different choices. When a colleague pleaded with me to take some time off and get the situation organized, I would have. When a counselor from the Division of Youth and Family Services reached out to support, I would've answered the call. Overwhelmed, stretched thin, and giving myself grace, I desperately wanted to hold onto the career I'd fought so hard for. The same career that was causing me to overwork myself and neglect home. Instead of taking time off, I took on more. Instead of seeking aid from appropriate resources, I went at it alone or looked for help from those who expected some form of reciprocation, which didn't work, either.

The center of the end came during the first phone call I made after my nephews were taken to foster care while I was at work. I was frantic and defeated.

"They shouldn't have been there anyway," I overheard my sister say. "If I wasn't in the hospital, they would never have been taken there. She can't do what we do on the regular with all these kids. She's just not built for it."

Hearing her assessment of me, I shattered. I assume she didn't see that the glass shield surrounding my heart was marked *fragile* before demolishing it with a sledgehammer. Suddenly, whatever respect I had for myself was drained; my sails were at half-mast. My confidence shaken, I felt I wasn't good enough for anything I was doing, so I completely checked out. I didn't fight for the money the state owed me for keeping the children, fell behind on rent, and lost my place. On top of everything else, now I had to find a place to stay.

In relocating, I blew through the money for the kids' extracurricular activities, and they were devastated when I delivered the news that I had to pull them out. Everything was crashing around me. I got so caught up in the chaos at home, that even when I decided to show up for work, I wasn't really present. I only half-performed and was eventually laid off.

By the end of the end, I was submerged in self-doubt, drowning in regret, and refused to acknowledge that I was severely depressed and that my mental health had been on a slow decline for years. Leaving work forced me to sit down and take a self-inventory, which helped me draw the conclusion that the people who were hurt by my arrogance and selfishness would be better off without me.

On the outside, I did the self-work it appeared I should be doing: applying for jobs, interviewing, mothering, co-parenting, and attending school to finish a BA/MA program. Internally, I was criticizing every word that came out of my mouth, every decision I was supposed to make, every idea for a paper, and shaming myself every time one of my children made a mistake. I was convinced my life was over. The worst part about my private reality was, it was the exact opposite of what I told the people who were trying to support me through my decline.

When you are caught in a self-destructive cycle, depression becomes a beautiful nightmare. Beautiful in the way that the negativity feeds your own belief system. Imagine that a combination of inevitable circumstances and your decisions have subconsciously convinced you that you aren't enough. That you're not worthy of love, or capable of giving love, even when you want to. Now that you are convinced, you do everything you can to confirm what you've already convinced yourself.

We exist by constantly manifesting what we believe, and because we believe it, we get comfortable. Depression told me comfort is beauty, even if it hurts. The people who love you start noticing the destructive behavior and try to help by doing everything they know how to. But when it becomes apparent their help isn't provoking change, they get frustrated. You want to receive their help and follow through and grow and change and do better for yourself, but the only thing you're comfortable with is the lie suggesting there is just something wrong with you. Sinking deeper and deeper into depression, before you know it, there is nothing you like about yourself, and you're unable to see the beauty inside of you, so you retreat from everyone to save them from you. During this part of the end, I slept for a year and a half.

When I finally woke up, I moved into a beautiful duplex in my hometown. I hadn't lived closer than forty-five minutes away for eighteen years--yet, there I was. The call to move back home came in the aftermath of months of prayer. I slept and prayed, cried and prayed. What if my family didn't welcome me? I had walked away so long ago that my friends, my ex, and my network were my support system--everything I built without my family.

What would they say when they saw how bad things were, I wondered. Of course, they'd ask questions, and I'd be forced to admit things I preferred to take to the grave. I wouldn't be able to withhold or play victim and would have to stand up all the way. I worried about going home to the tune of losing twenty pounds before we were settled into the new place. And then we were settled. And I told the truth. And no one ever even asked about the whys.

At the start of the beginning, God showed up through my village. The first layer of support was a connection to a mental health professional. I diligently performed the self-work I'd been running from, and my village showed up alongside me. They were there when I needed to talk, vent, or unpack the lessons I was learning. Slowly, I began understanding that the work I had been doing and the money I was making wasn't worth what I had to sacrifice in order to have it all. Once COVID hit, my connection to my children was reinforced, which helped me identify the areas where I could've shown up better for them. The time they've been required to be home has helped us see what's necessary to move from surviving to thriving.

In this beginning, I am walking with gratefulness, counting my blessings, and moving in righteousness. I'm standing tall in the knowledge that each decision I make, no matter how minuscule it seems, affects my life either now, or later. I understand that not choosing is a choice in itself.

When I look at how far we've come as a family, sometimes I ask myself how I missed the value of what I had before. Why didn't I appreciate everything when I was gainfully employed and living my best life? I think it's because I needed the ending of my old life to prepare myself for the life God has designed for me. I believe that God uses all things, even events that seem to be intended for our demise, as tools to help us blossom. Sometimes as I'm swaying in the breeze, I remember how badly the end hurt. These days though, I don't even wince. If this is just the beginning, I believe the best is yet to come. And the right now is pretty damned beautiful.

Faith, Food, and Fertility

CANDICE DAVIE

Getting Diagnosed

Growing up, I was a late bloomer. Throughout my school years up to college, I was the skinny girl with more intellect than curves. Judging from the women in my family, it was probably never in the cards for me to have double D's anyway. But that didn't stop me from wanting a body like Tyra Banks, which was a nightmare for a young girl who desperately wanted to be seen as more than the smart girl in class. To top things off, I had super oily skin, which was prone to frequent breakouts, and my menstrual cycles were all over the place, making an appearance every three to four months. At the time, I didn't mind because the last thing I wanted to do was deal with my period. Besides, doctors said my infrequent cycles were normal and would improve as I got older, so I just found ways to cope with it.

The irregular periods continued into my twenties, and I was prescribed birth control pills to balance my hormones. The breakouts also continued, and I assumed it was taking my body longer to "normalize." At 25, I was newly married and visited my gynecologist for an annual exam. The doctor asked various questions about when I wanted to start trying to have a baby, my medical history, and so on. Based on my responses and the symptoms I was having, she ran tests on me for a condition called Polycystic Ovarian Syndrome (PCOS). I'd never heard of PCOS before, so I had nothing to go off of besides what the doctor told me: if I were suffering from this condition, I'd have to take medication to regulate my body, and if I wanted children, I'd have to start fertility treatments.

Growing up, my entire life was planned out, complete with a very specific timeline and goals:

- Graduate college by 21.
- Married by 23, living in a white house with a picket fence.
- Birth my first baby by 26.
- Work as a pediatrician by 28.
- Second baby by 29.

Write and publish a few New York Times best sellers by 35.

Needless to say, most of my goals hadn't gone as planned. Obstacles came, adversity got in the way, and my plans were either tweaked or thrown out altogether. Through it all, I desperately clung onto my dream of becoming a mother. Motherhood was something I needed, like air; when my doctor called to confirm my bloodwork showed I did have Polycystic Ovarian Syndrome, it literally felt like I was suffocating. It was the death of a dream.

What is PCOS?

Polycystic Ovarian Syndrome is a condition that affects about five million women in the United States. It's a hormonal imbalance that can cause ovarian cysts, irregular menstrual cycles, ovulation issues, and fertility problems. PCOS can also cause other health problems, such as excess facial and body hair, acne, thinning hair, depression, or weight gain. Not all women who have PCOS experience all of these symptoms. On the other hand, experiencing some of the symptoms doesn't necessarily mean a woman has PCOS, which can be frustrating and confusing, especially when misdiagnosed.

The exact cause of PCOS is unknown, but many doctors think that it could be due to a number of factors:

- Genetics
- Thyroid disorders
- Insulin resistance
- Exposure to endocrine disruptors
- Being overweight
- Being underweight

Diet & Lifestyle

The first year after being diagnosed was especially hard for me. I cried. I prayed. I was wracked with guilt, believing I was being punished for an abortion I'd had a few years prior. My mind and emotions were all over the place! After a few days of throwing myself a pity party, I went into overdrive to find a way to see my dream through. The doctors' solutions weren't good enough; there had to be a way for my body to be healed.

I scoured the internet multiple times a day and came across tons of PCOS forums, blogs, and articles. It was overwhelming at first, but I was relieved to find I wasn't the only woman dealing with this issue. Tons of questions raced through my mind: *Which supplements should I try? Which specialists should I see? Is there anything that can really change my situation? Will I ever be able to have a baby?*

At first, I took all the medications my doctor prescribed without question, following the instructions to a tee. There was metformin to control my insulin levels, which can affect the reproductive system and hormones. Next was Provera–a form of progesterone to help with the irregular cycles. Then I took the fertility drug Clomid for about two months, hoping to get pregnant. However, the hot flashes, night sweats, and mood swings became too much for me after a few weeks, and I stopped taking it. My body was rebelling, and my marriage was quickly deteriorating. Each month when I retested, and the big, fat negative sign showed I still wasn't pregnant, I sank deeper into depression. I couldn't focus and felt like giving up on this whole dream…so that's just what I did.

At least temporarily.

After numerous meltdowns and too many days in bed to count, I had a mental shift. I'm not sure what caused it besides the fact that I was tired of feeling sick and tired. I needed a healthier, happier me. I stopped buying baby clothes every time I went to Target. I stopped staring at the room I imagined would be the nursery and stayed away from the blogs and forums that dominated my daily routines, making a conscious effort to change my thinking in order to change my life.

Instead of focusing on becoming a mother, I concentrated on my health, other goals and came to grips with the possibility I was fighting a losing battle against God's will for me. I was overwhelmed and on edge all of the time; all I wanted was peace.

First, I targeted improving my health. In late 2015, I listened to a podcast by Jess C. Lively, featuring Alissa Vitti, who had PCOS and was able to get pregnant naturally at the age of 37 through diet and lifestyle changes. She'd written *The Woman Code*, a popular book helping women follow a five-step protocol that could balance their hormones and take charge of their reproductive health. As I listened to her testimony, I ended up taking five pages worth of notes. I thought I'd been doing everything possible to improve my health, but when Alissa mentioned no dairy, very little to no meat (unless organic, grass-fed), and no alcohol, I realized there was so much more I could change.

A Mental Shift

If I wanted God to heal my body and bless me with the loving husband and healthy babies I dreamt of, I had to see it, truly believe it, and live like I knew it was coming in God's time. Believing it could happen for me meant learning how to heal from unresolved emotional baggage. I honestly didn't think I had an issue with this until I read how much resentment, anger, and unforgiveness can physically manifest through various illnesses and ailments in the reproductive system. I was forced to take a step back and examine my actions and demeanor. Was I holding onto something? Not a day went by I didn't think about how I'd gotten rid of the baby I would've had fifteen years before. Although so much time had passed, I was unknowingly dealing with more guilt, resentment, and fear than I realized.

Miracles Still Happen

In 2016, I began to see the manifestation of things I'd been praying and working tirelessly towards for years. In April 2016, I got engaged! It was what I wanted for so long but was never sure it would happen; with him, at least. I could not have asked for a more perfect and romantic proposal. I spent the next six months planning our beachside wedding ceremony in Florida, preparing for the next phase of our lives. November 20th–the day after my grandfather's birthday, everything was going to change when I walked down the aisle. And it did…sooner than I thought.

In the midst of wedding planning, I began feeling off. My stomach didn't feel right; I was extremely fatigued and seriously moody. Though I was concerned, I dismissed it as a stomach virus or a combination of going to bed late and waking up early. After a few days of feeling like crap, I stopped by the pharmacy on my way home from work and picked up a pregnancy test. When I got home, I took the test, then busied myself cleaning the kitchen and preparing something to eat while I waited. I didn't know what to expect, but when I went back to check the test, it was there: PREGNANT. I didn't believe it! I was pregnant—NATURALLY! No fertility treatments, charting, timing, or any of those things. One positive test went against everything doctors had told me for fifteen years. Fifteen long years! I was overwhelmed with emotions.

A New Journey

After I discovered I was pregnant, life seemed to move at lightning speed. Since I had PCOS and was 36 years old, I was considered high-risk. Severe morning sickness lasted all day for the duration of my pregnancy; I struggled between gratitude and depression. I was so sick; I could only go to work and straight home every day for months. It was the most isolating, mentally and physically draining time of my life!

In spite of going into labor three and a half weeks before my due date, I had a dream birth. Since I'd gone through so much through the pregnancy, I believe God spared me a long and painful delivery. After eleven hours of labor and four pushes, Benjamin Charles Davie was here. He was a little early, but he was healthy and everything I prayed for. It was truly surreal to finally look at the face of the baby I had asked God to bless me with for fifteen years.

Once my husband and I took our baby home, I realized that I wasn't ready for all the emotional and physical changes that come with motherhood. I had to set boundaries, especially when it came to family, friends, and even my career. A few weeks after giving birth, burnout and anxiety crept in. I quickly learned that sleep deprivation and not telling people "no" would cause me to want to escape from it all. My advice to new mothers is to do what works for you and don't be afraid to set boundaries. Your well-being should be top priority.

Live the Life You Want by Faith

Whether you are dealing with PCOS, endometriosis, unexplained infertility, or any other physical ailments, know you can be healed.

God made your body and has placed everything you need inside of you. Believe that God wants to heal you physically and emotionally and watch things begin to change. You are more than deserving of the life you imagine, but you can't do it alone. There was a time I was discouraged, depressed, and didn't think that the baby, loving husband, and other dreams I longed for were possible. I was doubtful and broken. Through my journey, God showed me I had to let Him help me, and when I did, He answered my prayers in ways I never could have imagined!

True Worth

CHANEL PRINCE

I grew up in a Christian household, where there were numerous restrictions. When I was a child, I didn't like being subjected to the rigid rules. It felt like I was being controlled and didn't have any freedom. However, as an adult, I've come to appreciate my upbringing and learned that the restrictions reinforced the morals and values which were being instilled in me. It laid the foundation for who I am in present day—a woman of God, more valuable than rubies and pearls.

Growing up, bullying and name-calling hurt my self-esteem. I heard so much negativity about myself; I eventually believed what people said about me. It wasn't just what people said, though—my parents' absence played a part in destroying my confidence as well. Don't get me wrong, my aunt did an amazing job raising me and showing me love. However, love from your biological parents is something a child longs for.

I sought love in the wrong places and recklessly engaged in sex in the hopes of finding it. Foolishly, I believed sex was a way for men to show the love I desperately wanted and used it as a tool to keep their interest. By the age of 18, my first son was conceived during a casual sexual encounter; he was born one month shy of my 19th birthday. Seemingly, in the blink of an eye, I became a teenage mother.

When my son was four months old, I met a man who became the love of my life for the next ten years. We hit it off the first day we met; his intellect, vocabulary, and etiquette instantly attracted me to him. We spoke daily and spent a lot of time together. Four months into the relationship, I discovered I was pregnant with my second child. I was ashamed because my son was only eight months old. I was scared of what my family and people at my church would say.

My family was shocked but loved my children and me nonetheless. My church family, however, handled the news very differently. I was called to a meeting which left me devastated. They forced me to apologize in front of the whole church and ask for forgiveness. I was beyond humiliated and eventually stopped attending church for a while.

In 2016, after years of living under my boyfriend's mother's roof, I finally moved into my own apartment. By then, our relationship was strained because he wasn't showing up like I needed him to. We had just welcomed another child; however, we hadn't been a couple for years—we just lived together and slept together. When I moved, he moved in with me, and we eventually got back together. It felt like when we first met—puppy love all over again. But everything changed when I found out he was cheating with his co-worker. The sad part is the woman knew of me but didn't care. Apparently, he didn't either, because he cheated with her while we were living together as a family. That hurt the most because he'd done the same thing off and on when we lived at his mother's house. I truly thought those days would be over when we created a home of our own. Sadly, I was mistaken.

Hurt and livid after discovering his co-worker's text message, I checked all of his social media accounts and installed a spy app on both of our phones to track him. Depression stole my appetite, and I lost so much weight. All because I wanted to feel loved again. The love I desired and deserved. I had let him back in my heart but was determined not to have sex with him to prove to both of us that I'm worth more than what's between my legs. I wanted to find solace in another man; however, I realized that having sex is just that—sex. It's also a transfer of emotions and soul ties. I was determined not to create any more soul ties. If I were to have sex with a man to get back at my boyfriend or even just for pleasure, I would end up hurting myself because I wanted more than that. I deserved more than that. Still, I ultimately went back on my word to myself, and my fourth child was conceived, fathered by my estranged boyfriend.

After having my daughter, I didn't view life the same again. She was the gift from God who opened my eyes. I was broken, shattered, depressed, lonely, and hopeless. I felt like I had no one to talk to or turn to; having her gave me hope and the strength to keep pushing. Before she was born, my world was turned upside down. My boyfriend lost his job a month before I delivered my daughter. At the time, I worked as a paraprofessional in District of Columbia Public Schools (DCPS) and wasn't paid during the summer. So, a few days after giving birth, my whole family and I went on daily runs to make money by working for Uber Eats. Can you imagine doing deliveries, breastfeeding and changing a newborn, and tending to three other children simultaneously? It was rough but had to be done so we could make ends meet.

The stress of it all caused me to suffer from postpartum depression and want to give up. So many days, I cried, sinking into a dark place, not wanting to be bothered with anyone. I constantly wondered why I got myself into this predicament. I had no drive to do anything; I didn't even want to return to work that Fall. Every day that school year was a day in hell. I hated where I was placed and felt like no one cared or understood.

When my lease finally ended, so did my relationship with my boyfriend. It was hard in the beginning because I didn't have a car. I had to make sure my two older children were at the old apartment complex to get on the bus each morning until the county assigned them to a new bus route. I took an Uber or Lyft to drop them at the bus stop, then dropped off my baby at her dad's house on the other side of town. Finally, my youngest son and I went to school and work. Thankfully he attended the school I worked at. But that didn't resolve the fact that I was about an hour and a half late to work for seven weeks until the new bus route for my older children was finally approved. I was relieved because I knew that the enemy was trying to get me to quit, but God made a way.

The first year raising four kids by myself started out very challenging, and there were many nights I cried myself to sleep. I didn't understand how I was going to make it by myself, but I kept faith in God the whole time. Again, he came through when my best friend gave me her old car. I was beyond blessed! Although the car had a few issues, not only was I mobile again, God placed a mechanic in my complex who often fixed it free of charge. To add to my blessings, that Fall, I secured a job with Prince George's County Public Schools (PGCPS), making much more than I did at DCPS. God continued opening doors for me that I thought could never be opened. He looked out for me time and time again.

In the process, I learned so much about myself and God. There is no love greater than the love of Christ. No man or anyone for that matter can ever love you like God can. You have to love yourself first and set standards of what you will and won't accept. Never lower your standards for anyone. We are worth all we believe we deserve because we're precious jewels. I used to think sex was the way to show love, but it's not. Love starts with loving God and yourself—loving your flaws, strengths, and everything in between.

By placing God as the head of my life, I have experienced a love I have never experienced before, and I'm content. I am still healing from years of not loving myself and allowing others to abuse my love; however, I am making progress with each passing day. When we move out of the driver's seat, God guides us, and everything we've gone through begins to make sense. I had to go through every encounter in my life to be who I am today. I may have felt helpless and hopeless, but looking at it now, I understand it all. God used my mountains to perfect His will and purpose for my life. I am complete because God is the author and finisher of my faith.

Through it all, I've learned no man or person can determine my worth. I had to recognize my value before anyone else could. I now know WHO I am because of WHOSE I am. I've come to love and accept me for me. I have flaws, but I embrace them. Also, I intentionally put myself first (after God) in all things and refuse to settle for less than I deserve.

Oftentimes, we devalue ourselves based on what we're familiar with, but settling keeps us bound. Complacency isn't the answer—it's a trap. The key is to let go and let God. Sometimes fear attacks our hearts and minds, making us doubt we can make it on our own. The truth is, the devil is putting those thoughts in our heads to keep us bound!

God can bring us out of it all. Change your life, open your heart to God. Say goodbye to complacency and being undervalued. Reject hurt, pain, depression, anxiety, and low self-esteem. Say hello to new beginnings, joy, peace, agape love, self-love, high esteem, and your true WORTH as the daughter of the Most High King!

I Open My Heart

CHARELLE BUTLER

This is a series of actual entries I wrote in my journal to help me cope during a dark season in my life.

January 2, 2017

God, You are the only one I know who can help me achieve success. I want to draw closer to You, Lord, not only this year, but for the rest of my life. Last year, I let worry and fear consume me on my job, in my finances, and even in my spiritual life–but not this year! God, I need You now like never before. I need You to show up strong and manifest yourself in my life. Make me invisible; help others see You before they see me. Anoint me from head to toe so I may think, talk, walk and act like You, Lord. Thank you for bringing me this far and teaching me how to pray for what I need. Teach me how to pray for others and to be who You created me to be. I want to do Your will, oh God! Teach me to love as You love. I know it will be difficult, but with Your strength, I will overcome. I love You, God, and I want to serve You. Teach me how to fight, even when I don't want to. Teach me how to believe, even when I can't see the outcome. You said You are working for our good in all things, God. Teach me how to eat the Bread of Life, which is Your Word. Teach me to forever chase after You, even when I'm tired. I'm Yours, God. Allow my life to be an example to others, both young and old. I praise You and thank You for the victory in advance. I love You, God.

Love always, your daughter,
Charelle Butler

February 2, 2017

"Get up, Charelle!" I thought as I laid in my bed, comfortable and warm. I didn't want to, but I knew I had to get up. I had to get ready to face the day, go to work, be an adult–the usual. So, I got up glanced at the clock, which read 6:30 a.m. As I walked to the bathroom and rubbed the sleep out of my eyes, I felt a jolt of anticipation. My menstrual cycle had yet to make an appearance, so I thought I should take a test to rule out pregnancy. My cycle had a habit of appearing whenever she wanted, so I didn't think much about what the results would be as I placed the used test onto the counter then washed my hands. After a few minutes passed by, I looked down, expecting to see a negative line; however, to my surprise, two lines appeared. It was positive.

"Wait, what?" I screamed inside my head. So many emotions overwhelmed me all at once: happiness, excitement, bliss, followed closely by doubt, regret, and of course, fear. How can I be pregnant? I wondered. I mean, I knew how it happened, but I couldn't wrap my head around why. Especially as a newlywed of only four months! Living with my in-laws and renting a room that barely had enough room for me and my husband, it was obvious that we couldn't afford to have a baby. Where would we even put the baby? All these thoughts ran through my mind, but like most people say, "If you want to make God laugh, tell Him your plans." So, I took a deep breath, swallowed my negative feelings, and celebrated the fact that I was going to be a mother.

My Mother

Myra Alesha Prince was my mother. My mommy, mother, mama bear, mama smurf; she was my best friend. We didn't share the traditional relationship that other mothers and daughters do, though. See, I wasn't raised by my mother–I was raised by her older sister, Aunt Faye, or as my siblings and I call her, Nana. My mother suffered from substance abuse, so I wasn't able to live with her growing up. Despite her flaws, I loved her immensely.

Mommy was diagnosed with stage three lung cancer in August of 2012. Naturally, I wanted to take care of her, so I moved to New York for a year to be with her. After months of chemotherapy and radiation, she went into remission, and I moved back to Maryland for a year. Unfortunately, in 2014, she was diagnosed with a brain tumor, and without hesitating, I raced back to New York. I wanted to be there for her as she endured intense physical, occupational, and speech therapy. I ended up staying with her another year, then moved back home to Maryland and got married.

When I shared the news of a new addition to the family, Mommy was overjoyed, which made me more excited and forced me to push down the fear that was rising as each day passed. In the beginning, I was in shock that I was pregnant because I didn't think it was possible, but I was truly grateful.

April 22, 2017

I was nearly three months along and enjoying my pregnancy. One day, my husband Aaron and I were attending our church's annual marriage retreat and preparing for dinner when I received a call from my mother. "The cancer is back" were the only words I heard. I went numb as if someone had knocked all of the air out of my lungs. "I love you" were the only words I could murmur as I tearfully ended the call.

Tears flooded my eyes as I tried to make sense of what had just happened. "Oh God, am I going to lose my mother?" I thought. A wave of grief washed over me, and I fell to my knees, sobbing uncontrollably. Aaron wrapped his arms around me and tried his best to console me as I struggled to find the strength to pick myself up. All I could think about was my mother and what she must've been feeling. I needed to be with her. "She needs me, and I need her to pull through this," I whispered. I still don't even know how I made it downstairs to dinner that night. I couldn't eat; I was too worried about my mommy to think of myself.

May 24, 2017

Life was a nightmare, and reality didn't seem real. It was like everything was moving fast yet in slow motion. I'd seen my mother twice in the hospital; she was diagnosed as terminal a week after she told me the cancer was back, and it spread rapidly through almost every part of her body. There were even tumors on her spine, which caused her chronic pain. She was advised she could take as much pain medication as she wanted to keep her as comfortable as possible.

The first time I saw Mommy, I didn't recognize her. She looked so frail and weak and wasn't able to feed herself. I sat near her bed with my face toward the window, so she wouldn't see the tears streaming down my face. I hate seeing the people I love in pain; it broke my heart to see Mommy like that. Her only request was to see her children, but my older sister Charrisse and I were the only ones who showed up.

When they told us Mommy would be moved to hospice, denial vanished, and reality took its place. "So, this is really it, God? You're really not going to save her?" I thought as I held Mommy's hand while she dozed off. I told her how much I loved her, and if she needed to go, she could go and be at peace.

The last time I saw Mommy, she was more lucid. It seemed like she was getting better, but that was just me in denial. She was talking more and cracking jokes like she normally did, but there were two things I'll never forget that she said to me as I sat next to her while she gently rubbed my hand. "You're gonna be just fine, Charelle. You have Nana and Julia, and most importantly, God."

I couldn't say a word; I just wiped away the tears rolling down my cheeks before she saw them. The last thing Mommy said to me shakes me to the core, even until this day. I was two weeks from my anatomy scan, which would reveal the gender of our baby, so needless to say, I didn't know what I was having. "I'm so excited about my grandson," she said with a smile. For a moment, I was confused because I truly thought I was having a girl, which would be my mother's first granddaughter.

"Are you talking about Charrisse's five boys?" I quizzed her.

"No, I'm talking about you," she replied. I didn't give it much thought then, but months later, Mommy's statement would ring true.

May 24, 2017, was the day my mother departed from this life. I remember every detail of that day. I worked later in the evening but woke up early that morning, terrified I was late for something, but I didn't know what. I didn't feel like myself; it was as if something was off. I didn't want to go to work but went anyway, completing one facial before asking to leave early. "I just feel like I need to be home right now," I told my manager. She let me go home without question.

I arrived home, feeling exhausted. I got undressed, crawled in the bed, and took a nap. Charrisse had stayed in New York to take care of our mother; she took her out of hospice, so she could go home and pass in peace. She called me every day to update me on Mommy's status, so any time Big Sis flashed on my phone screen, my heart dropped to my stomach.

When I woke up from my nap, I laid there for a moment, checking out the sun as it shined through the bedroom window on such a beautiful spring day. I looked up at the sky as the wind gently blew the trees and began praying. I thanked God for the beautiful day and everything He'd done for my mother. I reminded Him how graciously He saved her life not just once, but twice before, so I knew He was more than able to do it again. After all, He is the God of encores. I finished my prayer by saying, "God, if it's Your Will that she goes, give me the strength to handle losing her. Your Will be done God, Amen."

I don't think three minutes passed by before my phone rang, and Big Sis appeared on the screen. "Yeah, Relle, I think she's gone," my sister screamed when I answered the phone. "Ma! I'm calling her, but she's not answering. She's gone!" I don't know how to describe what I felt hearing those words. All the feeling left my body, then came back in a wave which literally brought me to my knees. I cried so hard, I made myself sick. Aaron tried his best to comfort me, but I couldn't grasp the horrible reality that my mother was gone. "I need my Mommy!" I yelled. "She needs me; I have to go to her now!" Darkness wrapped itself around me like a cloak, and I couldn't see past it. Little did I know, this was only the beginning.

June 5, 2017

It was a week after my mother's memorial service, and I was walking around in a fog. The service replayed in my mind like a nightmare I didn't know how to wake up from. I hated myself because when it was time to share a few words on behalf of Mommy, I went mute as grief seized my vocal cords. Instead of getting up to say something, I stayed glued to the chair. In denial and angry she was gone, my eyes stayed glued to the doorway to the funeral home, waiting for her to walk in as if everything was fine. Of course, that never happened.

It was weird trying to return back to life as usual. Confused and out of whack, I talked to my mother multiple times a day—before work, at work, and even on my way home. "How am I supposed to go on without her?" almost became a mantra for me. Quietly sobbing in the bathroom at work and home became my daily routine. I felt so alone.

At 20 weeks into my pregnancy, I went to see my OB for my anatomy scan. At times I forgot I was pregnant because I was so wrapped up in grief. Before my doctor started the ultrasound, I thought back to what my mother had said about me having a baby boy. Though I smiled, I wanted a little girl to name Myra in her memory.

As I anxiously laid back on the examination table for the doctor to reveal the gender, an eerie quietness filled the room. It was awkward and made me nervous. "Maybe she's just taking her job too seriously," I tried reasoning, but even that thought wasn't reassuring. Once the scan was complete, Dr. Fries instructed me to meet her in her office across the hall without revealing the baby's gender, annoying me even further.

I sat down across from her, searching her face for answers, nervous about how concerned she looked. "Your baby is exhibiting some serious development issues, dear," she said flatly. A knot formed in my stomach as she continued. "The heart hasn't formed correctly, and the brain seems to have some issues as well. It appears to be tricuspid atresia, a congenital heart defect. The tricuspid valve didn't form correctly, so the red and blue blood is mixing in the heart." She paused for a moment before pushing out a breath of air to continue. "I have to admit you to the hospital because you're dilated one centimeter already. We have to make sure you aren't in active labor."

My lips moved, but nothing came out. Air escaped my mouth as hot tears drenched my cheeks. "Are you serious?" I muttered. "My mother just died a week ago! This is too much," I wailed as my body went limp and my head fell into my hands. My mind refused to settle down as the room spun; I was seconds from passing out. Through the nausea and dizziness, I'd forgotten the doctor hadn't told me the gender of the baby yet. When I asked what the baby was, she casually replied through a pained smile, "It's a boy." "Mommy was right," I whispered.

I was admitted to the hospital for a few hours and found not to be in active labor, so I was sent home on pelvic rest. I wasn't allowed to have sex until after I gave birth and was given suppositories to put in every night to keep my cervix from dilating. Aaron picked me up from the hospital, and it felt like it took forever to get to the house. I wanted to sleep the pain away, but on the way home, I explained to him that I had to go to Children's National Hospital to get echo cardio ultrasounds about every three weeks in order to monitor our son's heart, and needed an MRI to check his brain activity as well.

As soon as I got home, I went to bed, but sleep never came. I lay awake thinking about everything that had come about and cried out to God, asking Him to heal my baby boy and restore him back to health. I asked God for the strength to endure and to comfort my grieving heart. After my prayer, I lay awake, wondering what my future had in store for me.

July 3, 2017

By July, my life was seemingly a series of bad events, with one bad thing after another slamming me. I was on my way to yet another doctor's appointment, which seemed to be all I ever did. Going back and forth to doctors, I barely worked, leaving everything to fall on Aaron's shoulders; another thing for me to feel bad about. The doctors at Children's Hospital confirmed our son's diagnosis of the congenital heart defect, explaining that as long as he was inside of me, he was fine, but once he was born, he'd have to undergo three surgeries: the first when he was a week old to put in a shunt, the 2nd to remove it at six months, and the last when he was a year old to redirect the blood flow in his heart.

In the midst of this, we were also faced with having to choose whether or not to continue with the pregnancy. The doctors advised that when a baby has certain development issues, some couples choose not to go through with the pregnancy, but I'd already fallen in love with him. He moved inside me; I knew he was there and didn't want to end his life because he wasn't "perfect." We were keeping our baby.

I was prepped for an amniocentesis test, a diagnostic test to confirm whether or not a baby has a chromosome abnormally. The results provided doctors with a better understanding of our son's defects. To administer the test, they used the longest and thickest needle I've ever seen in my life. They went through my stomach and pushed their way through into my uterus to retrieve a sample of the amniotic fluid. The pain was torture, but I pushed through for my baby boy.

Following the test, I was given an ultrasound to see how the baby was doing. He was well, but I was dilating again. The look on my doctor's face was the same as when I had my 20-week appointment–I wasn't going home. I was dilated to two centimeters and was in active labor; I was admitted again. I was numb emotionally and physically, but didn't feel any pain. I was put on a magnesium drip, and wasn't allowed to eat for 24 hours, and got a steroid shot in my thigh to help my son's lungs to develop fully.

I spent two days in the hospital. Being poked with so many needles made me think of my mother. I thought about all she had to go through and how brave she was, being strong not only for herself but also for others around her. Mommy was a woman who never let people see her sweat. I needed to be just as strong as her, not for myself but for my son. I put my emotions on the back burner, feeling like they weren't that important at the time. What was important was the life of my son. I needed him to survive.

When it was time to go home, Aaron and I waited in the hallway for my discharge papers, discussing baby names. After much back and forth, Aaron named our son Isaiah, and I gave him the middle name Myron after my mother's name Myra. Naming our son gave him more of a life and made him more real. We looked up the meaning of the name Isaiah: God is Salvation. Somewhere inside of me, hope started to grow. I believed God would make everything right. He saw all I went through and would take care of my son because he's a gift in the midst of our storm.

July 24, 2017

I woke early that morning to do my regular morning routine, contemplating whether or not I wanted to go to work. My days had drifted into work and doctor's appointments; emotionally, I was numb, but I honestly didn't mind that. Holding in everything was better for me and everyone around, so I prayed and left it in God's hands. This was His way of making me rely solely on Him. I surrendered to His Will and ended my prayers with, "Your Will be done." My faith and trust were solely in God's hands.

It was early, so I climbed back into bed for a few extra minutes of sleep. I decided to go to work, but I was going to treat myself to an Uber instead of walking to the bus stop. My bladder felt full, which was annoying because I'd just used the bathroom. As I rolled my round belly up, a sudden gush of fluid rushed between my legs. "Oh my God, I peed in the bed, and Aaron just washed the sheets!" I thought as I panicked, feeling nasty and utterly mortified!

I waddled to the bathroom to clean myself up and noticed I was still leaking fluid. I hopped on the toilet, aiming the "pee" in there, but I couldn't control it or stop the flow. I jumped up, stuffed a washcloth in between my legs, grabbed my phone, and called downstairs to my mother-in-love, Julia, who was in the living room talking to my sister-in-law.

"Ma, I'm leaking!" I yelled into the phone. Although I was panicking, she remained calm and said she would call the ambulance. After hanging up, I hurriedly got dressed, stuffed a towel up my sundress, then waddled downstairs, trying not to disturb the makeshift diaper I made. I was so embarrassed. It was July, and Isaiah wasn't expected to come until October. As I waited for the ambulance, I wondered what if my baby came now. I wasn't ready; we didn't have a crib, a baby bag, or even clothes for that matter. I couldn't hear myself think over the ambulance sirens, which arrived with a firetruck.

Those who know me well know I don't like to be the center of attention, so being carried out on a stretcher was mortifying. I hated the stares I got from our nosey neighbors and onlookers. I was grateful Julia came with me because I didn't want to be alone. I called Aaron and told him I was on the way to Washington Hospital Center. Children's Hospital was right next door, and Isaiah would have to be transported over there immediately once I birthed him.

I was admitted and placed on another magnesium drip before the doctors broke the situation down for me. "Mrs. Butler, you won't be leaving here until you have that baby," they said. "That can be later this week, or a week from now, but our goal is to keep you here. You're 28 weeks pregnant, and your baby has serious issues. We want to keep him inside of you as long as possible because that's the safest place for him right now. Our goal is to get you to 34 weeks, but if we can get you to 36, that would be perfect. "We want him to gain as much weight as possible to make sure everything else is fully developed. If he were born right now, the survival rate with his congenital heart defects is extremely low and makes the complications for both of you higher. We're putting you on magnesium to protect his brain from cerebral palsy, as well as to stop your labor. Because you're still leaking fluid, we're going to put you on penicillin, so no infection develops. From here on out, you are on pelvic rest as well as bed rest. You can only get up to use the bathroom and shower–that's it. We're going to get you compression boots for your legs to prevent blood clots from developing from being in bed all day. Do you have any questions?"

My throat was dry, and I fought hard not to break down. There was no way I could be in the hospital that long, so I requested bed rest at home, which the doctors quickly denied. My cervix was opened to almost 4 centimeters, so if anything were to happen to me, it would be best if I was already at the hospital. I understood the ramifications and everything the medical personnel were saying but didn't want to receive it. *What about my job? How was I supposed to help Aaron make sure that Isaiah had everything he needed once he got home?* Fear crept back in with a vengeance; life felt like a cruel game that I was losing at every turn. I was overwhelmed by feelings of abandonment, and fervently prayed. Not only was Isaiah's life in danger, mine was, too.

August 19, 2017

At 32 weeks along, I was miserable, lonely, and bored. I sat on my behind all day watching countless reruns on television and was restless from lack of sleep. Every three hours, my temperature and blood pressure were checked; every four hours, I was hooked up to a monitor for 30 minutes to check Isaiah's heartbeat. Unless I had to use the bathroom or take a shower, I was restricted to bed.

In spite of the inconvenience, it wasn't all bad. The nursing staff was polite and friendly. I think they liked me because I didn't bother them much. I only asked for water and ice every so often, and they gave me little snacks that I appreciated. What was annoying was the loneliness I felt. Even though church members, family, and friends visited me every so often, when they left, the silence was deafening. Honestly, it felt like I was in solitary confinement. Being alone with my thoughts 24/7 for an entire month nearly drove me insane.

At this point, I overthought everything, even the simplest text message from a friend or family member. Aaron visited me when he could, but I understood that with him being the sole provider, he had to take care of all our bills and expenses on his own, leading to less time for me. It hurt so much to see him working so hard, knowing there was nothing I could do to help ease the burden; however, God is faithful and sent so many people who helped us.

The assistance we received was a relief, but being alone made the old feelings I'd buried months before resurface. I cried more, my emotions were all over the place, and I was extremely unstable. I went from being happy one minute, to angry the next. Even my doctors picked up on it. At the beginning of my hospital stay, I was pleasant and smiled a lot because I wanted to make the best out of a bad situation, but as the days went on, I grew bitter.

Every morning, the doctors asked me the same questions over and over again. Sometimes, one doctor came in and was almost immediately followed by another doctor asking the same things. "How did you sleep last night, Mrs. Butler? Are you still leaking? Are you drinking enough water? Did you have a bowel movement today? Did you strain? How are you feeling?" Every single morning at 7:00 o'clock, I was hit with the same line of questioning. One day I was so angry, I answered, "No, I'm not getting any sleep! How do you sleep when someone keeps barging in here every three hours to check your vitals? How can you sleep when every three days, someone comes in to change your IV? How can I be happy when every four days, I'm woken up at 3:00 a.m. to have blood taken?"

The doctor went stone-faced, then replied, "I'm so sorry to hear that, Mrs. Butler. Would you like us to give you something to help you sleep at night?" I angrily brushed the tears out of my eyes and declined his offer as thoughts of my mother flooded my mind. I still couldn't believe she was gone. Even until this day, I feel as though she's on vacation somewhere, and I just haven't spoken to her. My heart ached for her, and I cried every day. I cried for the things I didn't get to say and for every emotion I held in. I cried until I was tired of crying.

One evening, Aaron spent the night with me, and my heart was so happy. We couldn't do much, but his being there was such a comfort. Late that night, I started having contractions. At first,

I didn't know they were labor pains; it felt like I had to urinate, but every time I went to the bathroom, there was nothing. My leaking got heavier, but I didn't think anything of it. I went back to bed, but when the pain grew worse, I knew it was time. "I think I'm in labor, Aaron." I wasn't sure, but I woke Aaron up just in case. "Then call the nurses," he said, reminding me we were in the hospital.

I called the nurses, who hooked me up to a heart monitor. Isaiah's heartbeat was strong but was going in and out. Without a word, the nurses moved me into labor and delivery. By the time they checked again, I was five centimeters dilated, and didn't have time to fully process what was happening. The pain started out mild but became stronger and lasted longer with each contraction and was consistent.

Despite the agonizing pain, I was calm and let my body do what it had to do. I'd planned to have a natural birth without pain medication, but let me tell you something: there's no book, no video, no breathing seminar that can adequately prepare you for childbirth. Once the pain hits, you want it to go away as soon as possible. Needless to say, I opted for an epidural, but because I was on penicillin, I had to wait until the bag was empty before it could be administered.

I stared at the bag, impatiently waiting for it to finish as I groaned, trying to catch my breath. I was placed on oxygen due to low blood pressure, which felt strange because I thought pain makes blood pressure rise. I guess I was different. While Aaron retrieved everything from my original room, the epidural was finally administered and instantly put me at ease. If they could be packaged into tablets, I'd buy them out of stock! I felt nice and was finally able to take a nap, but after a while, I felt Isaiah drop. It was time.

As the doctors and nurses prepped me to push, it felt like I was standing on the outside of my body watching myself give birth. It was amazing! In my mind, I was cheering myself on. Each time I pushed, I thought, "Oh my goodness, look at what my body can do! This is amazing!" It was a riveting and empowering experience. After nine pushes, at 12:56 p.m., little Isaiah Myron Butler was born. When my eyes met his tiny scrunched-up face, I fell in love all over again. I was a mother now, and Aaron was a father. As the nurses scooped my son away to be cleaned up, I heard him belt out one good cry, then silence fell. I frantically looked over the doctor's shoulder to see what the nurses were doing with him, then peered at Aaron to tell me what was wrong with Isaiah. Why wasn't he crying anymore? I panicked as tears fell from my eyes, wishing someone would tell me what was going on.

After what seemed like an eternity, the nurses emerged with Isaiah, wrapped up like a burrito, with a breathing tube inserted in his mouth. I asked the nurse if I could hold him, and she said no, but quickly changed her mind when she saw how stressed I was. She allowed me to hold him for two seconds. I still remember how he smelled, and how his little face looked annoyed like his mommy when someone disturbs me from a nap or something. "Okay, mama, we gotta go," the nurse said as she took him from my arms, then whisked him to the NICU, where he awaited transport to Children's Hospital. I felt so empty, like a piece of me was gone. I glanced at my empty stomach, wishing I still felt his kicks and turns. Darkness closed in, and my breathing was labored. No matter how awful I felt, I fought to stay positive for the sake of my son. He needed me to be strong.

August 25, 2017

We got the call the night before that Isaiah would be having his first surgery early the next morning and for us to make sure we were there to sign the documents. It had been a week since he was born, and I faithfully visited him in the hospital every chance I got. I pumped around the clock so Isaiah would have enough milk once he was able to drink it. I brought a cooler bag filled with my breast milk every time I went to the hospital.

When I arrived and saw him hooked up to all those machines and attached to all those tubes, my heart shattered into a million pieces, and I lost it. I got so frustrated with myself because I didn't want him to know I was crying. If he could be that brave and strong, then I could be twice that much. Even though Isaiah didn't really know what was going on around him, I still felt as though he was so brave. I rubbed his arms and legs, kissed his forehead, and gently assured him that he would be okay, and he'd be home with me and Aaron real soon.

Every night before I got the two hours of sleep I was able to get, I called to check on my son; my heart hurt when the nurses reiterated how sick he was. There was little hope that I'd hear a good report. His blood pressure was up and down, he wasn't peeing enough, and was retaining too much fluid. For the most part, he was sedated and given medicine daily to ease his pain. Once I was off the phone, I cried out to God, pleading with Him to save my baby's life. He was going through so much; I figured I was owed at least the happiness of him surviving this trauma, especially since I lost my mother four months prior. I closed every prayer asking for God's Will to be done, and for the strength to accept His Will for not only my son's life, but for mine as well.

It seemed like Isaiah's surgery lasted all day, but after a delay, it lasted six hours. We arrived at the hospital close to 7:00 a.m. and stayed until almost 11 p.m. Following the surgery, a surgeon advised us that there were more issues with Isaiah's heart than what was spotted in his echo scans. His coronary arteries weren't connected to his heart. His pulmonary artery was enlarged, and he still needed his shunt for the tricuspid atresia he had been diagnosed with.

Prior to his surgery, Isaiah went into cardiac arrest and had to be revived. Even after everything was repaired, he had to be hooked up to an ECMO machine, which does the work of both the heart and the lungs. Listening to what my child endured was devastating. My body went limp, and I sunk into Aaron's chest, weeping and crying harder than I had my entire life. Suddenly, anger rose up and replaced my sadness. *Why would God allow a child to suffer like that? Why did this frail, innocent human being who was barely beginning to live have to go through all that?* Even though the surgeon was optimistic about Isaiah's recovery, I didn't want to hear anymore. I was tapped out. I was done.

September 12, 2017

Isaiah wasn't getting any better. Slowly, his health was declining. He no longer looked like himself because he had retained so much fluid from being on the ECMO machine for so long. His limbs were so swollen, his skin started to tear. His fingertips and toes were black from poor blood circulation to his extremities. He was put on dialysis because his kidneys began to fail. There was a tube coming from his nose to excrete the bile from his body because his liver had begun to fail too. All of this was done to keep my son alive.

Regret consumed me. I blamed myself because I felt like Isaiah hadn't formed correctly in the womb. It was my fault; I'd allowed too much to fester inside me. I even regretted the choice to go through with the pregnancy after finding out about Isaiah's condition. What parent wants to see their child in agony? But we didn't know it would be this drastic and trusted that God would heal him.

On the Sunday before the 12th of September, I got a better understanding of the word healing. That Sunday, Aaron dropped me off at the hospital while he went to church. It was a beautiful day from beginning to end. The doctors were able to pull off some more fluid, so Isaiah looked much better than he had weeks prior. I spent the whole day talking to him, telling him how strong he was and how proud I was of him for making it this far. I even sang to him. Before I left, something beautiful happened. My son opened his eyes for the very first time and looked straight at me. It was in that moment I knew he was saying goodbye.

I can't describe the peace that overtook me. I placed my hand on his head and whispered in his ear, "It's okay, my love. Mommy knows you're tired. You can go now and be at peace. You are so brave." Isaiah looked at me and refused to look away. Tears tumbled from my eyes onto his little face, and I softly brushed them away. I kissed his head and his hands and told him I would see him later.

The next day, the doctor called us and told us he needed us to come in for a meeting about Isaiah and his progress. When I hung up the phone, I felt sick to my stomach. Even though I was still angry, I prayed. I mean, I prayed like never before. I prayed so hard, it felt like a blood vessel was going to bust in my head. I fell to my knees, said everything I wanted to say, and pleaded for a divine miracle. That's when the Holy Spirit spoke gently to my heart, showing me that healing isn't always what we want it to be. Sometimes, healing doesn't have a pretty ending.

On September 12, 2017, Isaiah Myron Butler received his complete healing. His major organs were shutting down; there was nothing else doctors could do. That day, Aaron and I made the difficult decision to let our son go. We asked our bishop to pray a prayer of dedication for Isaiah, as we were allowed to hold him for as long as we wanted. We held him until we watched him take his last breath. His tiny nose wiggled for a few seconds before his monitor went still. He was truly present with the Lord. Even though my heart was shattered, I was truly happy to see him no longer in pain. Through death, he was healed and made whole.

My Healing

For months following Isaiah's passing, I walked around in a fog of darkness. I hated the sound of laughter because I didn't feel like I deserved joy. Maybe I was being punished for something I'd done in my past. My heart had hardened; I didn't think God resided in me any longer, but the thing about God's love and His light is, it's infinite. It's something you can't comprehend. He will pull you out of despair, even when you're not looking for Him to. That is exactly what He did for me.

My mind was a battlefield. There were times when I didn't know how to mourn. There were days I welcomed death. I believed I had nothing else to lose but my life. I figured if I were gone, I wouldn't have to feel this pain anymore or be tormented by my emotions any longer. Although my friends and family were incredibly supportive throughout my entire journey, I needed something more. I wanted to understand why I had to experience this hurt, but I didn't know where to start. I was lost.

I use the Bible app on my phone from time to time because I love reading its devotionals. I started reading one called *Hope Heals in the Midst of Suffering*, about the story of Joseph. The devotional detailed how even through all his suffering, God had His hand on Joseph and raised him up. As I studied his story, I marveled at Joseph's strength. I learned that we don't go through things for ourselves; we can be a blessing to others while in the midst of our pain. I thought I had nothing to give because I was hurt by everything I'd gone through, but Joseph's story taught me that even when we are imprisoned in our own mind, God can still use us to be a vessel.

Allowing God to tear down the walls I built around my heart was a process. I had to accept being forever changed by the loss of my mother and son; however, I didn't want to be bitter, I wanted to be better. I asked God to forgive me for the anger I had towards Him and fasted and prayed for Him to soften my heart. I was tired of being angry and had to understand that through healing and releasing hurt, I wasn't giving up the memory of my mother or son, but receiving so much more. In place of fear, I received strength. In place of mourning, I received the spirit of thanksgiving. In place of despair, I received peace which surpasses all understanding. Did this happen overnight? Of course not. But it is something I experience every day.

God can and will meet us wherever we are in life. I'm living proof of that. He is patient and understands we are human before anything else. After all, He gave us emotions and wants us to feel each one of them. Most importantly, He wants us to be truthful about our feelings. In closing, I want to leave you with this: I once felt that God no longer lived in my heart, that my pain pushed Him out. But upon reading Romans 8:26-27, my faith was renewed. Nothing and no one can separate us from God's love. NOTHING. Even when we don't know what to pray at times, the Holy Spirit prays for us, and God listens! True healing begins when you open your heart to it. Keep your heart open.

The Blessings of the Battle

ILENE FERNANDEZ

In life, we all experience the kind of pain which can take us on an emotional rollercoaster, leaving us feeling as though we're suffocating with nowhere to turn. Drowning in mixed emotions, our anxiety increases as we turn to short-term coping mechanisms for relief. Oftentimes our pain goes through many phases before the healing process begins.

Life has taken me through many battles that have made me feel as though I was stuck in a never-ending tornado. One of the most unbearable hurts I've experienced is losing my mother. Learning to live without her has been like being reborn again. I don't think I'll ever fully heal from my mother's passing. But, over the years, I've learned to cope by remembering the wonderful times we've shared.

It all started in 2015 when things shifted unexpectedly. My mother's health began to decline, signaling what we were unaware was the beginning of the end. Initially, Mommy's sudden inability to maintain her balance didn't appear to be a major concern, especially when her doctor said she was experiencing vertigo and wrote a prescription to curb it. Life went on as usual as we did what we loved and spent time with each other. There were family outings, Broadway shows, and Sunday gatherings at my parents' house, where Mommy treated us to scrumptious home-cooked southern meals. However, as great as life was, everything took an unexpected turn.

There were days I was in high spirits, believing Mommy would get better. Then there were times when it seemed as if her health was rapidly deteriorating. By 2017, her condition worsened, and she was constantly falling. Every time I received a call that she'd fallen again, it crushed my soul. Between constant emergency room visits, appointments with her primary care doctor, and several neurologists, doctors couldn't identify the cause of her failing health. One doctor even admitted how strange it was that they couldn't figure out what was going on with her. In the meantime, she developed dry eyes, and even eating became excoriating for her. It seemed like everything possible was going wrong with her body.

My father was persistent in finding Mommy help and eventually discovered a neurologist who diagnosed her with Progressive Supranuclear Palsy, which came as a relief because maybe now she could be cured. I didn't understand what the disease was or why the test results were mailed instead of communicated in person, so I forwarded the results to a friend who worked in the medical field. After sharing the test results with the doctor she worked for, my friend advised me to spend as much time with my mother as possible because the prognosis wasn't good. Still, without a complete understanding of my mother's illness, I consulted the internet for clarification. The more I educated myself on the disease, I got dizzy, and everything became a blur. Tears drenched my face as I read there were no treatments or cure for her condition.

Although she was in the fight of her life, my mother remained strong. I wasn't ready to face this pain, but I tried to remain positive. I cried many days and nights, pleading with God for a treatment or cure to show up. But as time passed, Mommy lost weight, and it became difficult for her to swallow. She needed daily assistance but managed to push through for her family. So many questions clouded my mind: *How could the glue to our family fall apart? Why my mother? Why did she deserve this?* She was one of a kind—loyal, authentic, a great mother, wife, grandmother, daughter, sister, and friend. Of all people, she definitely didn't deserve what was happening to her.

While working full-time, mothering two little ones, and taking graduate school courses, I was forced to come to grips with my mother's illness. I still didn't understand how one person could endure so much. None of it seemed real until September 7, 2018. Each time I reflect on that day, I'm forced to experience the trauma all over again. I relive how I avoided the incessant ringing of my phone as my sister called me several times before I caved in and answered the inevitable. I knew the day had come, but I didn't want to face it. The exact words as my sister's distraught voice boomed through the line escape me, but the grim bottom line remained the same, my precious mother was gone. My soul shattered beneath the shock of the horrific news.

Mentally, I thought I was prepared for Mommy's death, but I wasn't. This was too much for me and my family to accept. We hadn't had time to even process the fact that she was gone before we had to make funeral arrangements, which only deepened the wounds. But as a family, we comforted each other through the heartbreak. Each of my sisters and I have been blessed with a piece of Mommy's strength; collectively, we used it to uplift our father and brother. Death can either bring families closer or rip them apart. Though we felt broken, our family bond was strengthened. It was painful; however, we kept the family traditions alive in my mother's absence.

My mother was the rock who always stood by my side. Our relationship was authentic and one of a kind. She was the best friend I could talk to about anything without limits. She nurtured, guided, and gave me strength. Most of all, my mother instilled the greatness which lives inside of me. SHE taught me how to be the phenomenal woman that I am today. How would I go on after losing the most instrumental person in my life? By the grace of God and with love from my support system, I got through this trying time.

Still reeling from my mother's death, my family and I were hit again. Seven months after Mommy's passing, we experienced loss again. My loving cousin passed away at the age of 42. Although I was grieving my mother, I pushed my pain aside to support my aunt and cousins. Why had my family been hit so hard? It felt as if we were under attack. I wanted this generational curse broken off! But more grief came before relief. On September 7, 2019, my family, friends, and I celebrated my mother's life and legacy. The morning following the celebration, our family was rocked yet again. My uncle unexpectedly passed after celebrating his sister's life. Even though I was devastated, I am grateful to have shared the last few hours of my uncle's life with him prior to his passing.

Knowing that my purpose in life had not yet been fulfilled motivated me to keep pushing through graduate school; I managed to maintain a 3.7 average despite my grief. On March 7, 2020, my loved ones celebrated me as I tearfully walked across the stage, proudly earning my degree. My mother was my biggest cheerleader. Her absence from my graduation left a tremendous void that could not be filled; however, I knew she was there in spirit. Also, her strength was very much alive in me. After all I had endured, I pushed through and accomplished my goal, just as she would have wanted.

The celebration was short-lived because I was dealt another hard blow when my significant other's mother's health began declining. This was painful for me not only because she and I had connected, but because I was once again watching someone I love endure excruciating pain, which caused my own suppressed emotions to explode. The day she passed, I discovered I was expecting. It wasn't the right time to deliver the news to my significant other, so I waited two weeks before presenting him with a baby announcement scratch-off.

He was elated by the news, but was sad that his mother wasn't there to celebrate with us. Still, at least there was finally going to be sunshine after the rain. I was so happy to get a break from grief until I was informed that I was miscarrying the baby after a few doctor visits. Not again! It felt impossible for me to grasp the right words to break the news to my children. It was easy to explain to my teenager, but how would I help my younger child comprehend the loss? Ultimately, I was transparent, and my children accepted that their sibling was gone.

Reeling from yet another loss, I yearned for my mother's shoulder to lean on, but I am beyond grateful for my father and siblings, who stepped up in her absence to comfort me. I also had a phenomenal support group comprised of friends and co-workers who assured me, "It is okay not to be okay." Their wisdom allowed me to release the feelings I'd buried, which became an essential part of my healing. Suffering a miscarriage is an unfortunate event that I won't ever forget, but it's one that I've healed from. Part of my healing was writing a children's book for other families dealing with miscarriages. It allowed me to repurpose my pain and help others heal too.

I've faced insurmountable battles, but I've found ways to push through the pain and transform those battles into blessings. For example, now I write to heal and help others. I've learned that with the adversity we face, if we move forward without discovering effective ways to cope, our healing becomes suppressed. Writing was one of my coping mechanisms. It allowed me to release what was bottled inside. It also allowed me to share my story to inspire others.

Self-care was another coping mechanism for me. At times, we get so caught up in day-to-day activities that we forget to take time for self-care. Neglecting to take care of ourselves can overwhelm us and cause us to crumble. I realized that I wasn't healing; I was merely distracted by life's happenings. I wanted healing, not a distraction, so I made an effort to practice self-care and check in with myself often. We must be honest and ask ourselves, "Am I healing, or am I distracted?"

We must diligently approach the healing process by setting intentions, executing, and leaning in for support as needed. When we understand where we are mentally, emotionally, and spiritually, we can embark on the journey to healing. Your best self is yet to come.

Grace and Endurance

JANICE COLBERT

My mother was the seventh child in her family; I am her seventh child. Wow, the 7th child of a 7th child! As a child, this revelation had no significance to me–I felt like just another in a number of children. However, as I've grown older, I've been amazed to see how God used the number seven throughout the Bible—where it represents perfection and completion. But growing up, I wasn't prepared for the significance of being the 7th child held.

My mother and I were extremely close and went through a lot together. We were open, honest, and transparent with each other. I saw her strengths and weaknesses, and she saw mine. No matter what I went through, Mama was always there encouraging me. People often complimented us on our beautiful relationship. She was my mother, best friend, therapist, prayer partner, mentor, advocate, teacher, and living example of a "Woman of God." She was truly a Proverbs 31 woman, the mother I wish every girl could have. I thanked God for her while she was living, and I still thank

God for choosing her to be my mother. God knew I needed a mother of her caliber to nurture me. She understood and accepted me as I was; she loved me like Jesus loves us, unconditionally and wholeheartedly.

God and Mama looked beyond my faults and saw ME. They were the only ones who understood, accepted and loved me with my flaws, imperfections, and all. They saw the best in me when everyone else could only see the worst. They loved me despite my mistakes or failures. I am the woman I am today because of Mama and her unfailing love for me. I thank God over and over again for blessing me with a one-of-a-kind mother.

My mother was my everything, and I am so glad I constantly told her this while she was alive. I always honored her, never hiding my love for her. I was proud of her as a Woman of God and a magnificent mother and wanted to make her equally proud. I never wanted to hurt or cause her any pain because of my conduct or disobedience. So, I strived to be the best daughter I could possibly be. I am the woman I am today because of God and Mama. She introduced me to God by how she lived her life. She was a living testimony, an example, and a witness. Not saying she was perfect, but she was saved, holy and sanctified. All my life, I aspired to be like Mama–she was my inspiration. When she went home to be with the Father, my entire world changed. My only consolation was knowing she was with the Lord.

Following Mama's death, I felt completely alone, hurt, and broken. I missed her so much; I couldn't even talk about her without breaking down. My days were empty, and my nights were long and lonely. I had no idea that her move to North Carolina was preparing me to learn to live with a permanent distance between us; God was already planning my life without her. As I think back, her move from New York seemed so final. Even until this day, I cannot describe why I felt that way.

Hating to see each new day after Mama died, I took a leave of absence from work because I was unable to perform my duties. Night's solitude brought relief because no one understood what I felt. My siblings' lives seemingly went back to normal, and my father remarried—which I felt was too soon after Mama's death. Life went back to normal for everyone except me. While they moved on, I sank into depression. The signs and symptoms were there. I craved solitude, didn't want to talk, and no longer had a reason to laugh or smile. I advised my pastor that I was taking a three-month sabbatical. He supported my decision and encouraged me to take as much time as I needed.

Months later, I returned to church, elated to be in the presence of the saints. As I walked down the aisle on my first day back, the Holy Spirit instructed me, "Sit where she sat." I stopped in my tracks and almost said, "I can't sit there!" But I didn't say a word as I eased into Mama's seat. Sitting there was different, but it felt good. At the end of service, the pastor called me to the altar and prayed for me, expressing what the Lord was saying. The healing process had begun.

From that day until now, the Lord has begun a new work in my life. He granted me temporary custody of my niece and nephew. I realized He gave me a responsibility so big I wouldn't lose myself in grief. Besides, Mama would have wanted me to move on and be happy. She and I had talked extensively about death and dying, discussing final arrangements and how we must live right so we can die right.

Soon, my days were filled with caring for the children. They kept me so busy, I didn't have much time to be sad. Our life as a blended family was filled with joy until it happened: the children were removed from my home because I didn't have separate rooms for each of them. Just as soon as my broken heart was mending, it was shattered again! They were crying uncontrollably, and though I was trying to be strong for them, I broke down, too.

That night, returning home without them, God took me by the hand and led the way. All these years later, it's still a blur, but only He can accomplish such a feat. Every time I thought about the children, I cried. I didn't get the chance to prepare them for such a traumatic upheaval, which seemed so heartless and unfair. For years, I've wondered if they knew the truth about why they were taken away, or if they've been told lies. God is still healing me from the devastation of losing them and the thoughts that subsequently planted themselves in my mind.

Later, I obtained custody of another niece who lived with me for a while and became my foster daughter. That got me to thinking that if I had a house, I could rear my nieces and nephews together since they are cousins. So, I elected not to return to work; I opted to foster my nieces and nephews instead of allowing them to go live with strangers. I soon was awarded custody of my niece's infant sister, and eight months later, their cousin arrived.

I was busy, with hardly any time to grieve and cry at night. God lifted my depression with the noise and laughter of the children that filled my apartment. My days were packed with activities, and the babies were thriving. Still, I longed for the first niece and nephew who'd been taken from me. I continuously thought about their well-being and where they lived. Finally, by the grace of God, we were able to visit them at the foster care agency. God is so faithful! We were so excited to see each other; they loved their baby sister and cherished her. Over the next few years, we had regular visits that we all looked forward to–it was like a family reunion!

My time of happiness was brief before being derailed by devastation once again. My eldest niece was a typical teenager who wanted to do her own thing. One day, she met up with some cousins and decided to spend the night. One night turned into five days…without my permission. Eventually, reports were made and reviewed, and the agency removed her from my home, placing her in a group home. I pleaded with them to no avail not to take her. Again, I was crushed.

I felt like I had failed my nieces and nephew, who'd been sent to live with complete strangers. My niece settled in at the group home, which I never considered home. In time, she visited us, and we were always happy to see her. She adored her baby sister, too. I don't feel she knows the truth about why she had to leave our house, because many people were in her ear who really didn't know the facts. But I thank God my nieces and nephews don't hold anything against me, and I am grateful for their hearts and compassion. It has been instrumental in my healing process.

As time passed, I continued healing from the loss of Mama and the children I lost to the system. God blessed me with the opportunity to care for three more nieces and nephews of various ages. Again, life was so busy, I didn't even realize that I wasn't crying myself to sleep at night or dreading a new day. Instead, I actually looked forward to seeing what it would bring. God was healing my shattered heart through the children. They were sweet, happy, truly a handful, and outnumbered me five to one. As they grew older, I had them do small chores like putting away toys, helping with their snacks, etc. My two daughters were my backbone and refuge during that season of my life and were the best support I could ask for.

Time was moving faster than I realized. I was a certified foster parent—the three girls were in pre-school, while the two boys stayed home with me. The children were doing extremely well and were as smart as can be. I adopted four of them and was fostering the fifth one. Once the adoptions were finalized, we moved out of state into a beautiful home. Although the kids adjusted and adapted well to their new environment, I didn't. I was lonely and missed my family in spite of us not being that close anymore, which made me miss Mama even more. I guess being in new surroundings made the pain resurface with a vengeance.

Though my heart ached, I faithfully walked the children to school each day, holding the pain inside. When I got home, I curled up in bed and cried. I cried so long and so hard, I believed I was losing my mind. A couple of hours before school ended, I forced myself to get up, take a bath, and headed back to the school to pick them up. I seemed so normal the children were oblivious to my affliction. But grief had taken its toll on me, rendering me helpless. Six months went by before I was able to settle down emotionally. God is so faithful, especially when you call on Him, admit your weaknesses, and acknowledge what's hurting you. He was steadily healing me–I was just too weak to feel it initially.

I had to let go and let God. It was time to reinforce my relationship with him—I needed fellowship and a church family. My entire family was brought up in church; church had been an important part of our life. So, when the children and I found a church home, it was a wonderful consolation. When I opened up my heart to God, the healing process went to a new level. I was happier than I'd been in a long time. But as most of us know, when God starts blessing, the devil starts messing. The adversary hates family because God created it, and regularly attacks it—mine was no different.

One evening, I went too far with my discipline of one of my nephews, who reported it to his teacher the next day. This prompted an investigation resulting in him being returned to the state we moved from. I'd already adopted the other four children and was considering adopting him too. But Satan brought on pain that hit harder than before when the decision was made to remove him from my custody. My nephew and I were practically up all night talking as I packed his clothes to prepare him to leave. I repented to him, begging his forgiveness. We were his real family, the only family he knew. How I wished I could turn back the clock. He simply peered at me with a slight smile and hugged me. "Nana, it's going to be alright," he reassured me. I was truly astonished when he said that, but I knew in my heart he'd forgiven me.

The next day at the airport was painful for both of us. He thought we were going on the plane together, and when he realized I wasn't going, authorities had to tear him away. He refused to let go of me. I was speechless, which is rare for me. He was running from the caseworker, fighting to stay with me, even though I was the one who hurt him. I felt like a huge failure for letting him down. It wasn't supposed to end that way. Honestly, I still feel some way about it. Only God understands, but I think I've finally forgiven myself. From that evening on, I've done a lot of repenting and praying to God, knowing He is a rewarder of those who diligently seek Him. Months later, the caseworker and foster mother asked me to come to visit him, which turned out to be marvelous. I visited a couple more times and called so he could talk to the other children on the phone. I missed him and wondered about his well-being. I'm forever grateful for his example of forgiveness and have learned to extend it to myself and others.

I've experienced so much hurt and so much pain. But God is my healer, and yours too. We can't heal from what we won't reveal. Don't let your past become your identity. God has healed us and forgiven us for our past, present, and future sins. Thank You, Lord!

My journey has been a long one; I experienced even more hurt along the way, but God has kept me. He used the brokenness in my life to make me whole. Through my hurt, pain, and brokenness, I got to know God the way I know Him now. My tribulations put me in the arms of God to be healed. I may have some scars, but I'm HEALED and BEING HEALED! It seems God gave the seventh children grace and endurance for their journeys.

The Almighty Power of Forgiveness

JULIA LONG

How do you forgive someone who doesn't apologize for their wrongdoing? Even worse, someone who denies ever wronging you in the first place. Is it even possible? Choosing to forgive someone who refuses to acknowledge the pain they've caused you can almost be as traumatizing as the offense itself. Forgiveness without repentance is difficult, but not impossible. How do I know? I'm a witness.

I was thirteen years old when the most heinous and unthinkable act was committed against me: a teenaged family member sexually assaulted me. Shockingly, it wasn't even on his own will—he was coerced into it by an adult we both trusted. The only explanation I can offer for a grown person forcing children to do atrocious adult acts is that they were under the influence of drugs. But even still, it was egregious behavior.

Unthinkable? Yes. Unimaginable? Definitely. Unforgivable? No. When I chose not to focus on the act itself, I was able to forgive and heal from that traumatic experience. Unbelievable, right? It truly amazes me that by the grace of God, I was able to forgive this person, although they don't even recall the events of that horrific day.

Unfortunately, that day was the first but not the last sexual assault I endured. Why was this happening to me? Did I have a sign on my forehead inviting predators to assault me? It was as if these people were granted permission to do whatever they wanted to me, and nobody would care. But I cared. The fact that it happened more than once convinced me I was all alone, and no one truly loved me. Without love, there is no trust. I couldn't trust anyone.

After each assault, I felt so dirty, afraid, and confused. Empty and defeated, I wanted to die. I felt so worthless; I attempted suicide more times than I'd like to count. What did I have to live for? Every day was an uphill battle. Out of fear and shame, I dealt with the pain of what happened to me in silence. I was tired of hurting and didn't want to live anymore.

Nothing I did in an attempt to take my life worked. Cutting my wrist with a butter knife and shaving blade failed. Swallowing pills to help me sleep forever didn't work, either. Why wouldn't God take away my pain? Before each attempt, I pleaded with Him to stop the hurt. He knew everything I'd gone through and experienced—what kind of God would let a child suffer like this? Didn't He hear my cries and my prayers? Did He care? Was He even real? I soon found out God is indeed REAL.

The last time I tried taking my life was when I took a handful of a relative's beta-blocker pills mixed with some other pills I couldn't identify. Almost immediately, my heart started racing like I'd just run a marathon. I began sweating profusely and urinating so frequently that as I got off the toilet, the overwhelming urge to go again forced me right back on. This was it, I was finally leaving this cruel world! I laid down and wrote a note to my father, explaining why I decided to take my life. Continuing the prayer I'd begun before popping the pills, I eventually drifted off to sleep. Hours later, my eyes opened to see my farewell letter next to me. What was going on? Why was I still alive? Why wouldn't God just let me go? There could only be one reason: I couldn't take my life because God had a plan and purpose for me.

The fact that I survived gave me a new lease on life. I slowly began doing things to enhance my quality of life, beginning with borrowing a book from the public library to study for my GED. I studied day and night and passed the exam the first time around, scoring high enough to be admitted to the University of Maryland. It was by the grace of God that I passed the GED exam, especially because I've always had learning challenges as a student.

While preparing for the GED, I also took skills development courses offered by the Department of Employment Services. I learned valuable skills like accounting, writing, and data entry. Additionally, I began working temporary positions where I acquired a tangible variety of skillsets. It turns out accounting was my passion, so I registered for college courses in pursuit of an accounting degree. Who would've thought that I'd go from willing myself to die to motivating myself to win? God was definitely in the midst of it all, revealing Himself through His works. I saw Him operating in my life, but I still hadn't developed a relationship with Him.

All of this changed after the summer of 1993. My cousin stayed with me for two weeks after beginning a spiritual sabbatical. Witnessing her spiritual awakening and conviction both amazed and troubled me at the same time. Her transformation seemed extremely radical, and I couldn't believe what she was willing to do to grow spiritually. In my eyes, her drastic behavior was borderline cultish. Her overnight metamorphosis didn't make sense, so I started reading the Bible to see if her actions aligned with God's Word. While I searched for contradictions, she stood her ground and continued walking with God. Intrigued by her tenacity, I began reflecting on my own spirituality.

I believed in God and that Jesus was the son of God. I also knew God had the power to save, but I wasn't certain if I was saved. I realized that I was saved by belief, though I had never made a verbal confession. Besides, my failed suicide attempts proved God actually answered my prayers and saved me. By all accounts, I should have been dead, but He saved me. I started reading the Bible, praying, and asking God to help me. However, this time, I wasn't praying for my life to end; I prayed God would help me live. I didn't just want to live, I wanted to be successful in every area of my life.

Soon I found myself visiting a local church. After a few visits, I gave my life to the Lord, sealed with my confession and baptism. I was so excited to be a part of something that was greater than myself! I loved my new church home and attended regularly. One day, I was listening to the radio when I heard an advertisement for a relationship seminar offered by another local church. Desperately wanting to improve my relationship with my family and husband, I immediately signed up. It was the best decision ever; the seminar was life-changing! I was taught that to build healthy relationships, we must understand where we come from, our environment, and our experiences. This revelation prompted me to consider how my past experiences affected my relationships.

I was living in my past. Trauma from my childhood led to trust issues, among other things. How could I trust anyone when I'd been hurt and violated by so many others, including those I'd least expect it from? People were wicked and untrustworthy, wolves in sheep's clothing. My walls went up. I operated from a place of protecting myself in my relationships, letting people as close to me as I felt comfortable. Believing I was setting boundaries, I placed conditions on my relationships, but in actuality, it was a defense mechanism to help me feel safe.

I also struggled with unforgiveness, strongly resenting the people who had hurt, harmed, and violated me. They meant nothing to me–if something bad happened to them, I wouldn't have cared. I wanted them to hurt as bad as I did and pay for what they'd done to me. I didn't hide my disdain, anger, distrust, or resentment towards them, openly expressing how I wished them harm and death. The seminar changed my point of view regarding forgiveness. No matter the circumstance or situation, we must forgive. In Matthew 18:22, Jesus commands us to forgive "seventy times seven." The Bible also says in Matthew 6:15 that if we do not forgive others, we will not be forgiven.

I wanted and needed forgiveness, so I had to extend forgiveness to others. With all that I had gone through, it wasn't an easy feat by far, but it was necessary. As a Woman of God, I wanted to live and apply His Word to my life. One of the sessions discussed forgiveness and why it was so important for us to extend it. The act of forgiving isn't for the other individual...it's for you. Scripture tells us that God will not forgive us if we do not forgive others, so I challenge myself to intentionally forgive. In spite of all the trauma and abuse I've endured, I forgive those who've wronged me, whether they show remorse and repent for their actions or not.

During the seminar, we also tackled human nature. Life experiences play a part in who we become. This is why victims often become victimizers. As the saying goes, "Hurt people, hurt people." I choose not to see them as predators; I look at them as broken spirits. The fight is not against flesh and blood, but against spirits and principalities. We can't view situations through the natural realm only–whatever is going on in the spiritual realm manifests in the flesh. For example, my loved one who violated me was operating under the spirit of addiction. Knowing this has allowed me to forgive because it was the broken spirit, not the person who harmed me. Addicts are bound to the spirit that controls and guides them, not a sound mind.

This mindset has allowed my heart to heal. In sharing my testimony, I want readers to know that it is possible to forgive someone who has committed a grievous act against them, no matter how horrific the pain. GOD is the answer; a relationship with Him is key! I pray my testimony helps someone else get through the unthinkable and seemingly unforgivable.

Father God, in the mighty name of Jesus, I give You thanks for this day and this work. A day of reflection of Your healing power! You have repaired my relationships with others and healed me in ways that far exceed my imagination. I've learned that I can love without judgment and without holding anyone hostage to wrongs against me. Through You, I can release the pain and truly forgive, even though I cannot forget. You took the pain, and I'm free! I'm free to love hard, free to care enough to tell my story, and free to give You praise, for You gave me strength when I was weak. You gave me comfort when I was afraid. You gave me peace when there was chaos, and now You have given me a love that comes from peace. I will give praise and glory to Your name forever. Hallelujah, Amen!

Broken

LAURA DULIN

It's so easy for people to tell someone to leave an abusive relationship, but what they fail to realize is just how difficult leaving really is. I spent ten and a half years in an abusive relationship with my children's father because leaving him didn't seem like an option at the time. In hindsight, I can see how my reality was controlled by his idea of who I was and who I should be. It was a toxic relationship that needed to end, but I wanted to be loved, even if that "love" meant losing myself. So, I stayed against my better judgment.

When I met him, I was a senior at Delaware State University. I'd just spent five months in New York with my mother, who'd been diagnosed with stage four colon cancer. I took time off from school to care for her, but when her health stabilized, she and I decided I would return to school for the spring semester. Although I was worried about my mother's well-being, a part of me was excited to get back to my college life. I missed my friends, the parties, campus life, and the freedom that I gained being away from home.

The day finally arrived for me to return to Delaware. Early that morning, I woke up anxious to use the one-way bus ticket which would get me back to the life I'd built there. Sensing my excitement, my mother was on me about leaving the house on time. While I was elated to get back to college life, I still worried about what may happen to her in my absence. However, I eventually pulled myself together and arrived at the bus station with fifteen minutes to spare before my bus departed.

With a little extra time on my hands, I grabbed a bagel and tea while I waited. That's when I noticed him stroll into the bagel shop. As he placed his order, I thought to myself, "Damn, he's cute!" But when he turned my way, I quickly averted my eyes to the book I'd been reading. He sat at one of the nearby tables to enjoy his food while I got up and walked over to the departing terminal. I sat on my suitcase, reading as I waited to board the bus.

Minutes later, the cute dude from the bagel shop was standing in front of me. I was so into my book, I didn't notice him until he said, "You dropped your ticket." I looked up with a smirk, brushing off his "pickup line," and went back to reading. "I guess you don't want to get on the bus then," he said. That's when I saw my boarding pass lying on the ground. It must've fallen out of my book. Embarrassed, I softly thanked him, and he flashed the prettiest smile. We boarded the bus and sat next to each other, talking for the next three hours about any and everything until I reached my stop. We exchanged numbers and promised to stay in touch. Little did I know when I exited that bus, my life would never be the same.

It was only a matter of weeks before he was in Delaware, practically living with me. Our relationship was intense; he seemed to always want to be around, and I wanted him with me. I fell fast and hard, ignoring all of the red flags, especially the first one that came up when I introduced him to my mother for the first time. She looked him straight in the eyes and said, "You got a lot of sh*t with you, G. That's your name, right?" Puzzled, he insisted that he didn't, but as they say, mother knows best.

Ironically, a few weeks later was April Fool's Day. He was supposed to visit that morning, but I couldn't get in touch with him as the day went on. Worried something was wrong, I called for hours without a response. Eventually, a friend of his called to inform me he'd been shot during a fight and was hospitalized in Virginia. I called my mother in hysterics to tell her what was going on. After she called him a few times, he answered and admitted it was all an April Fool's joke, and he was fine. He immediately called me to apologize and let me know he was on the road to see me, so I foolishly put the cruel prank behind me and eagerly awaited his arrival.

The second red flag showed up two months into our relationship. We were attending an event on campus when my phone rang displaying an unknown number. I ignored it the first two times, but after the third time, he told me not to answer it. Of course, that was my cue to answer the call. When I answered, I was greeted by a woman, calmly asking me if he was with me. Confirming that he was, I asked who she was to him. That's when she dropped the bomb that she was his wife and had just given birth to a little girl the day before! His April Fools' antics now made sense. He played a "prank" to cover up his disappearing act, escaping to be by his wife's side as she gave birth to their first child. My heart dropped. He snatched the phone and demanded she tell me the truth because he loved me and wanted to be happy. When he handed the phone back to me, she explained that their marriage wasn't official because he used an incorrect social security number on the application, and that they only married for the sake of a higher military paycheck. I should've walked away then, but I convinced myself that hearing their marriage wasn't real from her own mouth was reason enough to stay with him. Too bad I couldn't see the hold he had on her too; she was simply saying whatever he wanted her to say.

The following year, they had another baby together, and I would spend the next ten years entangled in his web of lies. Within the first year of our relationship, everything changed for me. Those things I was so excited to get back to in Delaware slipped away without me even noticing. Every time my friends invited me out, he made plans for us to do something else instead. If I insisted on going out with my friends, he'd make me feel guilty for choosing them over him. What good woman chooses her friends over her man? I wanted to be a good woman by his standards, so I stopped choosing my friends and chose him every time. Every day, I found myself at home, school, or work while he ran the streets or left town for days at a time. According to him, he was getting money, but our piling up bills begged to differ.

Every hidden secret eventually surfaced, and I wasn't prepared for what would be revealed. There were countless women, too many for me to detail. With each affair, I lost a piece of myself.

My self-worth was rapidly diminishing. I thought being a college girl with my own car, apartment, job, and tending to his every need made me a prize, but I was wrong. I tried proving my worth by doing anything he asked of me and even did things he didn't ask. Still, it wasn't enough to be rewarded with the love I deserved. Instead, I was seemingly punished. Minor disagreements would turn into physical altercations. It started with a push or pull, but as time progressed and I accepted it, the abuse escalated. He once choked me until I passed out, right in front of his friends. On another occasion, he hawked spit in my face. Even still, I sacrificed so much of myself but got nothing in return but abuse, hurt, and heartbreak.

The relationship began taking a toll on my health; I miscarried eight babies. Not as a result of a medical issue, but because of the level of stress I was under. Of all the miscarriages, losing our twins was the hardest. At nine weeks, I told him I was in extreme pain, but because of my previous miscarriages, he dismissed my concern as paranoia. I convinced myself he was right until a week later, when the pain became unbearable. He was preparing to leave town when I raced into the bedroom in tears, telling him the pain was so excruciating, I couldn't wait for my next doctor's appointment to be seen. Anxious to leave town, he blew me off and told me to just lay down. I begged him to stay home and take me to the hospital, but he refused and left in my car!

After a few hours, I couldn't tolerate the pain any longer, so I called a friend to rush me to the hospital. I tried calling him to let him know what was happening, but he didn't answer the phone. After hours of being in the hospital, scared and alone, the doctor informed me that my pregnancy was ectopic. One baby was growing in my right fallopian tube, and the other was in my uterus. Continuing the pregnancy would be life-threatening, so I was advised to terminate it. By this time, I finally received a call that he was on his way home and would get to the hospital as soon as he could. Before he arrived, the doctor advised me that I tested positive for chlamydia; the ultrasound showed scar tissue, indicating I had it for a while, undetected.

"How did you get that? I didn't give it to you!" he said when I told him about the doctor's report. I wanted to scream, but I just laid there and cried. An hour later, the doctor returned to administer a methotrexate shot to induce a miscarriage, then gave us explicit instructions–particularly my significant other. The doctor specifically told him the next week was crucial and that he should stay close by my side in case my tube ruptured because I could bleed out within minutes. As expected, he didn't heed the doctor's warning, and within two days, told me he was leaving town again. I reminded him the doctor said not to leave me alone, but he insisted I'd be fine, saying I knew how to call 911 if anything happened. Before he left, I went to the pharmacy to pick up my prescription since he claimed he didn't have time to do it for me. However, he had the nerves to ask me to stop at Home Depot to get a set of keys made on my way back because he'd lost his. When I got home, he was waiting in his car, I gave him the keys, and he took off.

Later that day, I checked our phone records and came across a number I wasn't familiar with and dialed it. The woman who answered claimed she'd been with him at our house earlier, then launched into graphic detail to prove they had sex on MY living room couch. Even in my condition, he selfishly sent me out so he could bring her into our home. When I told her I had chlamydia, she boldly told me she was the one who gave it to him. I was floored but stayed with him in the hopes things would change. Unfortunately, everything got worse.

That wasn't the last miscarriage or the last woman; these events became the norm for me. Over the next few years, he habitually cheated and blamed me for his straying. To numb the pain, I started smoking weed and cigarettes heavily to calm my nerves. To make matters worse, my grades took a severe hit from all the drama, and I stopped attending class. I couldn't focus on anything because I was too busy thinking about what he was doing in my absence. My mind would play out complete sex scenes starring him and some mystery woman, and I was paranoid he'd sleep with any woman he came in contact with. I smoked weed all day in the hopes of losing touch with reality, because my reality was too painful to deal with.

Three years after meeting him, my mother lost her battle with cancer. The last six weeks of her life were difficult. Having already lost myself, I couldn't stand losing my mother, too. I pretended to be fine in her presence, but she discerned how much I was hurting. I couldn't bring myself to tell her what I was going through because it would literally kill her. Knowing the day when I'd never be able to see her face or hear her voice again was quickly approaching, I wanted to spend every second of every day with her; however, I still chose him over her most of the time.

I don't know how I made sense of it, but when I wasn't with him, I felt sick. I couldn't sit with my mother too long because that would give him the opportunity to be with another woman. Three days before she died, I sat beside my mother and apologized for letting her down. I asked if she was worried about me, and she opened her eyes and nodded yes. I cried and told her not to worry about me because I would be alright. Sadly, I didn't even believe it myself, but I wanted her to be at peace.

The night before she died, I told him I was going to see her. "I'll drop you off," he said. My stomach dropped. My intuition told me he was going to use my time with my mother as an opportunity to be with another woman, so I asked him to visit with me. But he refused, saying he didn't want to see her in that condition. He dropped me off, and I spent the entire visit wondering what he was doing. As badly as I wanted to stay with my mother forever, I needed to make sure he wasn't out with someone else. So, after a few hours, I called and asked him to come to pick me up.

The next morning, I was jolted from my sleep at 6 a.m., with the sudden urge to visit my mother again. I went to wake him and noticed a big, bright red hickey on his neck. I wanted to die! My mother was barely hanging onto life, yet I was so consumed with trying to prevent him from being with another woman, I took her final breaths for granted. He wasn't consoling me or reassuring me things would be okay; he cheated on me instead. I left the house, heartbroken again. Hours later, my heart shattered into tiny pieces as my mother was pronounced dead. That was one of the lowest days of my life. I lost time with her that I couldn't get back because I chose him while he was busy choosing someone else.

The summer following my mother's death, things between him and me began improving. Following numerous miscarriages and dealing with him having three children by other women, I was finally pregnant without complications. I inherited some money from my mother, so we decided to take a much-needed vacation on a cruise to Mexico. We enjoyed each other and our time together. For the first time in our relationship, I felt like we were heading in the right direction; however, my optimism didn't last long. After returning home from our cruise, I intercepted a text message from a woman to him, commending him for his great performance on the last night of the cruise. I called her and asked the extent of their relationship, and she explained that she met him in the club on the ship and didn't know he was with his girlfriend. Once again, I wasn't enough.

The last night of the cruise, I'd gone to sleep early because of pregnancy sickness. I remember him coming into the room and snuggling up behind me in bed. He said he loved me, and that we needed to book another cruise as soon as possible. I kissed him and went back to sleep. Speaking with her, I realized why he was in such a rush to cruise again so soon. After hanging up the phone with her, I felt betrayed and worthless. I had just taken him on an all-expense-paid vacation, was pregnant with his child, and was doing anything he asked of me. Still, he cheated on me.

After spending days crying and rationalizing why his cheating was once again my fault, I decided I wasn't doing enough and needed to do more. I gave him full access to all of my bank accounts, allowing him to buy anything he wanted at his own free will, showed him more affection, and did whatever I could to make him happy. A few weeks later, he planned a trip for us to Florida, and I happily went. Again, I convinced myself he was sorry and put the not-so-distant past behind me.

Our trip to Florida went well, but a few months after the trip, I decided to get the disposable cameras from our trip developed at the Rite Aid down the street from our house. It was going to be an hour before the photos were ready, so I ran a few errands in the meantime. Upon returning to the store, I was confronted by a young woman who appeared to be about the same age as me, who said she developed my film and demanded to know how I knew her boyfriend. I stood there with my hand resting on my baby bump, absolutely confused as she went on to detail the extent of their relationship and how she'd gotten pregnant by him too but had an abortion two weeks prior because he changed his number and was nowhere to be found. How much more could I handle? Nothing I did for him mattered. After years of changing everything about myself for him, he constantly lied, manipulated, and never changed his deceitful ways for me. I was hopeless and stuck.

We stayed together and went on to have three more children. My role as a mother became my world. I was no longer fun to him, so he came and went as he pleased, sometimes gone for days on end. There were times when the kids and I were in the house with no food, money, or car to get around. Most days, I felt so lost; I didn't understand how my life ended up this way. I'd often cry and was drowning in depression. My family tried to be supportive, but it was no secret that they didn't like him, so I pulled away from them. I didn't want anyone to see the hell I was living in. There were many nights I called him nonstop to get him to come home, but he sent me to voicemail. However, if I wanted to do something alone, he told me that I was a bad mother or would have the kids call to ask why I didn't want to be with them. I'd hear him coaching them in the background, telling them I didn't love them, and I would hang up feeling like the scum of the earth. I eventually stopped going out alone and had no life outside of my children, but I couldn't say the same for him. He continued to live life on his own accord—disappearing, cheating, and doing as he pleased.

There was one woman he fell in love with. I sensed something was going on because he picked fights with me and disappeared for days at a time. He spent two days with her during the holidays, then came home early Christmas morning, acting like everything was normal. Meanwhile, I'd spent the three days prior sick because he was gone. I was hurting so bad, I contemplated leaving my kids and killing myself. He came home with hickeys all over his neck and didn't bother trying to hide them. Instead of asking about it, I found comfort in the fact that he was home for Christmas. That day, the kids took pictures of us laughing and playing as if we were the perfect couple. The smiles were fake; I didn't know if I was coming or going. I looked in the mirror and couldn't even recognize myself. I was depleted and didn't know how to fight for his love and attention anymore.

As the months went on, he treated me worse and worse. He was blatantly and outright disrespectful, telling me she was better than me, I had no hustle, and that I should be like her. After all the years I spent with him, everything I gave him, everything he took from me, and all of the children I lost because of him, how could he not see that he was my world? Things got so bad, he started beating on me more and more. I couldn't understand why he was treating me like this. All I could do was question what I was doing to make him act this way.

One day we got into an argument, and I told him I was going to pack up the kids and start over without him. He grabbed the gun he kept in a basket in the living room bookshelf, put it to my face, and told me I wasn't taking his kids anywhere and that he'd kill me before letting me be with someone else. He threatened me like that many times before, but never with a weapon. I was terrified, angry, hurt, ashamed, and confused. I thought about calling my brothers, cousins, and uncles to come handle him for what he had done, but instead, I pleaded for him to stop treating me so badly. I asked who she was and what she looked like, and he calmly responded, "She's better than you," and left.

Shortly after that altercation, I found out I was pregnant. I knew I couldn't have another baby, so I told him I wanted an abortion, and he agreed. He told me the name of the abortion clinic and where it was located. I questioned how he knew so much information about this clinic, and he said a friend told him about it. My gut told me he was lying, and he was. Two weeks after having the abortion, I went for my follow-up appointment. Before the doctor completed my exam, a social worker pulled me into her office, advising me they conducted a routine STD test on me; I tested positive for chlamydia. I couldn't believe this was happening again. I called him with the social worker on speakerphone, and he insisted she needed to run the test again because he didn't have anything, then hung up.

I went home even more broken and triggered because of the twins I had lost years before. As hurt as I was, I didn't even try to leave. Instead, I asked him to take a trip with me to Georgia to look at houses. I wanted to get him away from her. I wanted my family. I didn't endure all I'd gone through over the years just to walk away.

While we were in Georgia, I managed to get into his phone while he was sleeping. I pulled up a string of text message exchanges between him and the woman he was cheating on me with...in addition to videos of them having sex. The messages said he didn't love me but couldn't leave because I would take his children. As I read through their conversations, my body shook uncontrollably. The tears flowed, and I wanted to throw up. I eventually mustered up the courage to call her, and she told me she'd just had an abortion as well—at the same clinic where I had mine. She was pregnant again and wasn't going anywhere until they figured that out.

On Mother's Day, I decided I had enough. He was at her house, and I was home with the kids. I remember looking from my children to the holes in the walls from our many fights and decided I was leaving before he came back home. I took the kids and went to Delaware to stay with friends. He quickly moved her into the home we shared. Unfortunately, my move to Delaware didn't go as planned. Not only did I feel like I failed as a girlfriend, now I was failing at being a good mother, the one thing I was proud of. I was officially stripped of any worth I had left. Lowering my pride, I called him for help, and he came to Delaware and found us a house within a few days. He made sure to remind me that I wouldn't make it without him. He was right, I tried, and I failed.

Calling him for help came at a price. He and my father pulled a scam on innocent people looking to rent a home, using my brother's house to pull it off. When news of the scam got out, my family turned their backs on me, thinking I was aware of what had been done. I was losing everything and didn't know what to do or where to turn. All I wanted was to find a home for my children. I was so ashamed; I'd chosen a man who constantly gut-punched me and never considered the effects of his actions.

Although he moved to Delaware with us, he maintained his relationship with the other woman, traveling back and forth to New York to spend time with her. Two homes, two lives. One day, while in Delaware, he saw a text on my phone from a friend asking how the children and I were holding up. He confronted me, asking who my friend was and why was he texting me. Even after I explained that it was just an innocent text, he went crazy! He came out of the shower just to attack me. I ran out of the house, and he chased after me around the car butt-naked until he caught me. He dragged me by my hair as I kicked and screamed and instructed my two sons (who were three and one) to call me a hoe and a b*tch. I begged him to stop because I hadn't done anything to deserve that, but he continued with the assault. His last punch caused my jaw to lock up. I thought it was broken.

This brutal assault woke me up so to speak. I didn't know how I was going to get out of this toxic relationship, but I knew I needed to because my life depended on it. I ended up back in New York at my grandmother's house. Thankfully she allowed my kids and me to stay with her. He had warrants for the landlord scam and couldn't be around me. That time apart helped me realize I didn't deserve what he was doing to me.

After several months apart due to his warrants and three months of incarceration, he called, promising to be different and vowing to do better. He claimed the time and distance made him value what he had in me. I hesitantly took him back because I finally had my own apartment, was handling everything on my own, and started working as an assistant teacher for the NYC Department of Education. Truth was, I still loved him and wanted our family to work. When he came back, things were good. I never found out about another woman, he was respectful, and he told me that it was because of my love for him that he learned how to love.

He did well for about a year but then started hanging in the streets more and more. The weather was breaking, and he couldn't control his appetite for money. As much as I tried, neither could I. I decided to go back to school and transferred to Queens College for summer classes. On my first day of class, he dropped me off and picked me up. I didn't see him again until the next day when he returned home. I was pissed. Here I was doing something to better myself, and on the second day, he didn't show up, so I couldn't go to class. I told him he wanted to see me fail and that he never allowed me to better myself. There was no excuse for not coming home other than being dead in a morgue.

Three days later, he was dead. Murdered in cold blood on July 3, 2015. Seeing his body in the morgue, facing my children, being newly pregnant with our fourth baby, and spending the last ten and a half years with him left me completely broken. I was utterly lost. I spent my pregnancy in a fog, routinely making it through each day just enough to make sure that I didn't lose my baby, our baby. After giving birth, I decided that I had to rebuild myself, my life. I had four children depending on me, so I had to make something of myself.

I relocated to Delaware and enrolled in school at Delaware State University to finish out my undergraduate degree. In addition to school, I began working out and reciting positive affirmations every day. I felt happier and stronger each day. I maintained a 4.0 GPA throughout the year and was selected to participate in the Honor's Day program. I was also presented with the "Perseverance and Resilience" award. I was thriving, and so were my children. I was living a life that for so long, I only imagined. I graduated with a B.A. in English and secured a teaching job by the start of the school year. I also enrolled in a master's program. I was becoming the woman that I was destined to be.

The road to healing was a long, challenging one. But I held onto my faith, spoke life over myself, stopped being the victim, and allowed myself to live. Some days were better than others. At one point, I fought depression and sought mental health services. Therapy was instrumental in helping me on my healing journey. In 2020, in the middle of a global pandemic with a newborn baby and four other children, I graduated with my M. Ed in Secondary Education. Everything he told me I couldn't do, everything I convinced myself I was incapable of, I've proven to myself that I can and will continue to do. Most days, I smile and remind myself about my promise to my mother. I told her that I would be okay. I'm better than okay–I'm blessed.

What's Shaking?

LENA DEGRAFF

I was raised Catholic. Baptized, Holy Communion, confirmation, going to confession, the whole bit. However, as an adult, I never considered myself a religious person. In my humblest opinion, no matter what you believe in (Islam, Judaism, Hindu, Buddhism, etc.), as long as you're a decent person, you are of God. I consider myself spiritually grounded: I believe in God, and I know the Lord watches over me. I pray every morning as soon as I awake and open my eyes. I thank God for my many blessings; then, I pray for my family and friends. All of that changed, though, when I lost my parents within the span of a year—losing them tested my faith. I was angered by their loss and couldn't handle the hurt I felt, so I shut God out of my life.

My family isn't perfect—we've had our share of ups and downs. But the one thing I was always sure of, I was loved. I could always count on my mother, father, and bonus mom, Linda, who were my foundation and my rock. I have so many fond and not so fond memories of them. As a child, teen, and even as an adult, I was corrected and chastised by all three of them. Throughout my life, they helped me become the woman I am today. I couldn't ask for better parents and a better support system.

Linda married my father when I was ten. She, my mother, and my father had their differences, but they put them aside when it came to me. My senior year of parochial school is a prime example. One day, my father called to tell me he'd fallen on hard times, and I'd have to attend a different school for my last year because he could no longer afford my tuition. I cried my eyes out to my mother, who called Linda. Together, the two of them devised a plan to pay my tuition. I was beyond grateful for their great sacrifice.

Linda was truly a second mother to me and was always there for me. I loved spending summer vacations with her and my father. My father worked long hours, so I spent most of my time with Linda, which afforded us the opportunity to bond. We went shopping, watched movies, and visited the beach and the amusement park. We also talked about life—she always gave me such sound advice. I loved her dearly.

Linda had the mouth of a sailor, and I loved it. She must have rubbed off on me because sometimes I can be somewhat raunchy. I'd call her, and she'd say, "What's shaking, girl?" Then I'd tell her what was troubling me. If someone upset me, she'd asked if I wanted her to handle them. I'd laughed and tell her it wasn't necessary, knowing she wouldn't hurt a fly, anyway.

There was one particular conversation we had following my divorce that has stuck with me. I told Linda I was dating a guy who was fifteen years older than me, and she hit the roof, dropping quite a few "F" bombs. Even though my father was 20 years older than her, Linda didn't want me to follow in her footsteps. She said she loved my father, but as he got older, they weren't able to do as much as they used to. She wanted to travel and do the things my father had done when he was younger. Now, he just wanted to relax at home. Every time we spoke, she asked if I'd broken up with that old a** man. "Girl, don't do it to yourself," she warned me. Eventually, I saw what she was talking about. I wanted to hang out, and my man wanted to stay home. His children were adults, and mine were very young. He didn't want to raise more kids, so I let him go. Linda was so happy when we parted ways. I was grateful for her transparency and the insight she gave me.

I had a few rough moments throughout my life, but my world changed forever when my mother was diagnosed with ovarian cancer. I called Linda to discuss my feelings and vent about how hard it was to watch Mommy go through chemotherapy. Although it should have been a relief when my mother's cancer went into remission, I couldn't fully celebrate because Linda was diagnosed with uterine cancer. I couldn't cry on the shoulders of the two people I leaned on the most because I was trying to be strong for both of them.

I prayed hard for them every day. One thing I truly learned through this experience is that the stages of grief are real. I bargained, was angry, and felt guilty for not spending enough time with them or not being able to help more. Through it all, I prayed they would be healed and was elated when they both went into remission. I made plans to spend more time with them and love on them more. I treated my mother to her dream vacation in Hawaii and visited Linda and my father for Thanksgiving. I was grateful they were doing well; however, my newfound joy only lasted a little over a year.

In the summer of 2017, my bonus mom's cancer came roaring back with a vengeance. Her doctors informed her there was nothing more they could do and referred her to hospice care. Around the same time, my mother's cancer returned. While she was given medication to control the growth, I flew to Ohio to say my final farewell to Linda. It was so hard seeing her that way. She was hurt and angry; there was so much she wanted to accomplish that she would never get the chance to do. The strong-spirited lady I admired was helpless, and there was nothing I could do for her. I spent a few days with her, and it hurt my heart to leave, knowing it would be the last time I would see her alive.

Linda died on Christmas Eve in 2017. Instead of grieving her, I kept my feelings bottled up and focused on taking care of my mother and father. After Linda passed, my father and I grew closer. Normally, we spoke briefly for a few minutes, then I would spend hours talking to Linda. After she passed, he and I spoke faithfully every day at 9 a.m. If I didn't call him, he called me.

Sometimes I asked, "How are you feeling?" His answer consistently came back, "With my fingers," and I'd laugh. Or I'd say, "What's up, Pops? How are ya?" He simply replied, "Swell!" causing me to smile. Often, we had meaningful conversations about life, then would laugh and joke with each other. Pops laughed like Count Dracula and hearing it made me automatically burst into laughter. I enjoyed our budding relationship.

When he said he was moving to Florida, I helped him in every way I could. My sister and I researched various retirement communities and flew him to Florida to check them out. In the process of finding him a new home, we really bonded. Growing up, my father was always so stern and authoritative; now, he showed a silly side I'd never seen before. It was refreshing to see this lighter side of him.

Pops' birthday was in June, and I was determined to surround him with as much love as possible since it would be his first time celebrating without Linda. My sons and I drove to Ohio to visit him. I'll never forget the time we spent together. I wanted to take him out to eat for his birthday, but he made us breakfast instead since he preferred good home-cooked meals. We enjoyed a nice meal alone at his kitchen table, chatting for hours about his life, things he enjoyed, and his downfalls. He explained that he wasn't perfect, never drank or smoked, was a hard worker, and believed strongly in education. According to Pops, he only had one problem, he loved women. My father had ten children with five different women, but the one thing I can say is he never denied any of us and was always there when I needed him.

I will forever cherish our conversation that morning. Pops said that out of all his children, I was his number one. I was always there for him, and he counted on me. A week after our visit, he went to stay with one of my sisters in Florida until his apartment was ready. He was really excited about the move, and I was excited for him. I sent him everything in preparation: comforters, silverware, shower curtains, etc. Unfortunately, Pops never made it to his new apartment. A week before it was ready, he had a massive heart attack and died the same morning.

I couldn't believe it. I spoke with him at 9 a.m. the day before and asked how he was feeling. "With my fingers," he replied as usual, then said he'd been feeling a little under the weather, but now he was swell. He chalked it up to Florida's heat and said he needed to drink more water. Since he brushed it off and was feeling better, I didn't press the issue and chatted about other things. I even jokingly told him I was going to buy him speedos to wear to the community pool and teased him about how he was going to drive the elderly ladies wild. We both laughed so hard. I promised I would be there to help him move, but the next morning I was devastated when I received a call that he'd been rushed to the hospital and was unresponsive. By the time I booked my ticket to Florida, Pops was gone. August 8, 2018, will forever be etched in my memory.

I was shattered. Pops left me at 82 years young. "Don't worry, I am going to live until 100," he loved to say. Logically, I knew that no one knows when it's their time, but secretly I believed him because he was so driven and determined in everything he put his mind to. I felt silly for believing him. As bad as I was hurt, again, I couldn't fully grieve. I put on a façade because I didn't want my mother to see how bad I was feeling. She was having complications, and a CAT scan showed she had tumors throughout her abdomen. Trying chemotherapy once again, she couldn't hold anything down, and her abdomen continuously filled with fluid. After enduring the excruciating treatments for so long, my mother finally decided she didn't want to go through it anymore. I was hurt because I felt like she was giving up. But we had a heart-to-heart conversation where she revealed she'd had a good life with no regrets and was ready to go.

My mother had insurmountable faith. She believed in God, eternal life and was sure she was going to Heaven. I was with her from the beginning to the end. Although I initially felt like she was giving up, I quickly realized that having the level of faith she had is the strongest ability anyone can have. So, while I respected her wishes, I continued praying for her in the hopes she'd receive a miracle. I assured her that whatever decision she made, she had my support.

Some of my siblings kept trying to push Mommy to fight, but I stepped in and told them it was her choice. We brought her home so she could go in peace, surrounded by her loved ones. My sister flew in to help take care of her, and we took turns sitting with her and getting whatever she needed. It was really tough watching such a vibrant person deteriorate.

My mother was a truly remarkable woman. I've learned that sometimes we take for granted the blessing people in our lives truly are. When I arranged for a priest to come to the house to administer her last rites, Mommy ended up praying for him. He sat with her for over two hours talking and disclosed that he was going through medical issues of his own. Later, he told me that even though he'd come to comfort her, she turned around and helped him. He said she was a great person, and he would never forget her. That was the kind of woman my mother was and the impact she often had on others.

The morning Mommy passed, I was sleeping in the recliner beside her bed, dreaming. She and I were on a terrace near the beach, looking out on the water, soaking up the sunshine, and watching the waves. She told me she loved me, that I needed to do more with my life, and I should discover my purpose. I never got to ask her what that was because my sister woke me up, telling me it was time. I often wonder if that was truly a dream or a message from my mother. She died peacefully at home, February 7, 2019, surrounded by her children. Through a stream of tears, I read all of her favorite Psalms until she took her last breath.

That day was the last time I picked up a Bible for a whole year. After Mommy passed, I lost my connection with God. I was so hurt and broken that all of my parents were taken away, I even stopped praying. I couldn't understand why they were taken one after the other, and on top of that, I was burdened by a great deal of guilt. Had I been a good daughter? Did I cause them stress, or did I contribute to their happiness? Did I do enough to show them how much I loved them?

When I found out Mommy was diagnosed with cancer, I put her on a strict diet and prepared healthy meals for her: fresh, organic fruits and vegetables, lean pieces of meat, fish, and herbal teas. Everything was steamed and baked; processed foods and sugar were eliminated from her diet. She was doing well; however, I found out she had my brother buy her single-serving pies and processed cheese. He'd sneak her all the things I tried to keep from her. One day as we consulted with a nutritionist, Mommy complained that I wouldn't let her eat her favorite foods, so the nutritionist advised me to let up on her. Well, I relaxed, but a few months later, her cancer was back after being in remission for a year and a half, leaving me wracked with guilt. Although I'm no longer plagued with guilt, I often wonder if she would have lived longer had she continued eating healthier.

Towards the end of my mother's life, the weight of the world was on me. Every time my phone rang at work, my stomach dropped, scared it was time for her to go. I couldn't focus; my hands shook terribly, and I cried uncontrollably. I couldn't sleep and suffered from debilitating anxiety attacks. Nightmares haunted me as I tried to keep busy instead of dealing with what was going on with me emotionally. So often, in the Black community, we're told to keep pushing through without seeking help because of the stigma attached to mental health. After Mommy transitioned, I started seeing a therapist once a week. We dealt with my emotions, and she encouraged me to take time off of work to sort things out mentally and emotionally. Every time I saw her, she asked if I'd taken time off yet, and I made up countless excuses why I couldn't spare the time. Truthfully speaking, I was avoiding my feelings, but my therapist pushed the issue because she recognized I was at my breaking point.

I finally took the leave I needed, and my road to healing began, starting with increasing my therapy sessions to twice a week. I learned quite a bit about myself during our sessions. See, my mother played multiple roles in my life. We were so close; I lost more than a mother—I lost my friend and companion. We did everything together: shop, travel, and enjoy Broadway shows. Once she died, my hope went with her. I was so sad, I stopped praying; I was angry with God. How could He take my loved ones from me? He took all of the people I relied on for comfort and advice.

Therapy helped me realize I needed to take better care of myself. I couldn't be an asset to others if I was a hindrance to myself. I was running around trying to make everyone else happy, but there was no one taking care of me. I had to relearn to love myself. I was an empty shell, portraying to the world that I was okay while falling apart inside. Each Friday, I came home from work, peeled off my clothes, and stayed in bed until Monday, only getting up to eat or go to the bathroom. In hindsight, I was depressed. I emptied myself for everyone and everything else, but I had no one to fill me up.

My therapist related to me as a mother and woman, but it seemed like she couldn't relate to me as a Black woman. When I raised concerns I had about raising Black sons, I don't think she truly understood. She also didn't seem to understand the idea of the strong Black woman, nor how our family relied heavily on each other. Her response was to basically cut them off. While she couldn't relate to me on many levels, she did teach me a valuable lesson: I learned how to say no without explanation. If someone asked me to do something I didn't want to do, I simply said, "Nope, it's not happening." It was so freeing; I didn't once feel guilty about it.

I thought of Linda and how she gave her all to her family, yet denied herself the simplest of pleasures. I stopped waiting on other people and focused on what I enjoyed, what interested me, and started dating myself. I took myself to the movies, out to dinner, and traveled solo. I also set monthly hair and nail appointments and treated myself to massages. I even tried a few hobbies. The only thing I wasn't doing was praying. I had lost my faith.

One day, I was going through some of my mother's belongings and stumbled across some notebooks. Mommy was always writing. I thought she was studying her numbers because she liked to play the lottery, but to my surprise, I uncovered beautiful prayers she'd written. There were prayers for her children, grandchildren, family, and herself. I was both touched and amused by this discovery. I hung a couple of the prayers on the wall in my bedroom and living room. Reading them restored my faith. No matter what Mommy went through, she always had faith and trust in the Lord. This caused me to evaluate myself and my beliefs, and why I was so angry with God. The anger subsided as I realized death is the natural order of things. We eventually lose our parents and loved ones; we're not here to stay forever.

I remember thanking God for my parents, the memories we shared, and allowing me to know their love. I was reminded of Mommy telling me that we only need faith the size of a mustard seed, so I made the decision to reconnect with God. From that day forward, every morning, I thanked Him for allowing me to see another day and asked Him to bless me with a great day. This went on for months. Gradually, I started opening the Bible, and whatever I landed on, I read. I prayed more and more for my family, friends, and the world. How blessed I was to be able to reconnect and communicate with God!

Through this process, I've learned that as time passes, pain lessens. We just have to trust the process and feel with our fingers each day, as my Pops loved to say. I still have moments when I cry, but they are few and far between. I do my best to remember the good times I shared with my parents and bonus mom. I'm also now aware that I don't have to be a strong warrior Queen at all times; it's okay to let my guard down and allow myself to feel what I feel. Linda taught me that when it's time for me to make my final curtain call, it's important to know I gave life my all without regrets. I've also learned that there's a need for therapy, preferably with a Black therapist. We have to remove the negative stigma of mental health in our community. The greatest blessing in this experience is my faith and love of God are restored, thanks to my Heavenly angel, my mother.

Life After Death

MONICA L. WHITING-HOGANS

I will never forget May 11, 2017, the day my life was ripped apart. This was the day that began the testing and trying of my faith. It was on this day I awoke to discover the love of my life, my husband, Neil Christopher Hogans, had died.

Neil and I were high school sweethearts and friends; however, after not speaking since 1988, we rekindled our friendship in 2011, when he sent me a Facebook friend request. Initially, I wasn't going to accept the request because we hadn't spoken in so many years. But after contemplating for a few days, I finally hit confirm. Within seconds, Neil sent me a message, and just like that, we were chatting like twenty-three years hadn't gone by. Shortly after we reconnected, we went on our first date, and I challenged him every step of the way. After all, I was a 40-year-old, single woman with no children. I was hoping to get married, so he had to work to win my heart.

Neil definitely won my heart! I mean, any man who cuts his hair for you is a keeper. Let me back up: Neil wore his hair in long cornrows. I know, right? A 40-year-old man wearing braids. They were impeccable but wasn't the style I envisioned for the man of my dreams. I told him if he wanted a serious relationship with me, the braids had to go. To prove his commitment to me, on June 17, 2011, Neil cut off his braids. We were inseparable after that; when you saw Neil, you saw me, and vice versa.

Our love story was filled with peaks, valleys, and hurdles. The first hurdle occurred in May of 2012 when Neil had a stroke. By the grace of God, it was caught early, so there was no severe damage. He recovered well, and on November 2, 2012, Neil proposed to me. Most women cry when they're asked for their hand in marriage. But not me, I laughed and laughed! We had a ball planning our wedding, and on November 16, 2013, before God and a host of family and friends, we declared our love and sealed our union with a promise to love each other until death do us part, officially becoming #TeamNemo.

Neil was a diabetic, and in April of 2016, we learned that his kidney function was declining. By the end of that year, we had to decide whether or not he'd go on dialysis. Before taking the plunge on such a huge life change, we took our first international trip to Barbados, choosing not to dwell on his health and what was down the road. We walked into 2017 with bated breath regarding his surgery date, as well as securing a kidney donor for a kidney transplant.

Those first few months of 2017 were grueling. Neil begrudgingly opted to have peritoneal dialysis so he wouldn't be regulated to going into the hospital multiple times a week. We had to ensure everything was sterile; there were times I couldn't even be in the same room with him while prepping to make sure he wouldn't get an infection. Throughout all these challenges, my prayer life never wavered. If anything, my faith deepened, and I consistently talked to God without fail. Things seemed to be going well despite the circumstances. But without warning, a stream of unfortunate events triggered the beginning of my life changing forever.

On Friday, May 5th, we attended a formal affair with our family, friends, and church family—dancing the night away, celebrating my mother. That Sunday during church service, Neil took ill, and I rushed him to the V.A. hospital in the Bronx. Frequent visits to the hospital had become a part of our regular routine for evaluations and check-ups, so even though that day felt different, it was still the norm. A couple of days after being admitted, Neil was discharged and sent home. The next day, he called me at work to inform me he was out running errands. Can you imagine my anger? He'd just been discharged from the hospital and was already out running the streets. I was livid and planned to deal with him when I got home from my meeting that evening.

Besides being a wife, I also mentored teenage girls. Wednesday evenings, I usually went to my program with the girls, but that night God spoke to me and said, "Go home and be with your husband." I'm so glad I listened. I arrived home and cooked one of our favorite dishes—sausage and peppers with thin spaghetti. We ate and watched television as Neil told me about his day. I felt the heat rising on my neck as I sat quietly, listening to him. My anger swelled hearing him nonchalantly talk about running in and out of stores so soon after a medical crisis. When I couldn't take it anymore, I let him have it. We argued so badly, it got to a point we agreed to end the night in silence. However, even though we weren't speaking, we kept our promise to always kiss each other good night, no matter what.

Because he snored loudly, Neil always let me go to bed first. As he tucked me in with a goodnight kiss, I never imagined it would be the last one. During the night, Neil's snoring woke me up, but I tried to ignore it. Unfortunately, his snoring was louder than ever, so I grabbed my pillow and went to the living room. Sleeping in there wasn't out of the norm; many nights, I slept on the sofa until the wee hours of the morning before sneaking back into bed as if I'd never left, just to get some rest. Neil knew I did this, and it gave us both a laugh. This particular morning when I woke up and snuck back in bed, I was greeted by deafening silence. Have you ever experienced silence that's peacefully quiet, but eerie at the same time?

"Oh, now you stop snoring," I joked, but Neil didn't say anything. He just laid there with a smile on his face, or so I thought. I walked over to his side of the bed, touched his arm, and noticed how cool it was. I assumed he was cold because the window had been left open the night before. But when I saw the calm smile on his face, that's when I knew the love of my life was gone. I didn't want to believe it, so I called Neil's nurse and 911. Per the EMT, Neil had transitioned in his sleep. The coroner also confirmed that he'd gone into cardiac arrest sometime early that morning.

Can you imagine my guilt? Was Neil really snoring, or was he fighting for life? All I know is I left him alone because I wanted to sleep. It all felt so surreal. I refused to believe Neil was gone. *Had I said the wrong prayers? Did I not pray enough? Had I complained too much about how challenging his illness was, how tired I was of the doctor's visits, sterilizing everything, seeing him in pain? What could I have done better or differently to have my Neil here with me?* For months following his death, I agonized over those questions.

When Neil died, we'd only been married three and a half years and were just getting the hang of married life. Why God? I didn't want to hear any of the clichés. Oh, I'm sure you've heard them: You loved him, but God loved him more, He's in a better place, God needed another angel, Keep busy as it gets better, and so on. I didn't need to hear all those things; I needed my husband! I was so angry at God; I was almost furious. I stopped going to church and stopped praying, even though I was still having conversations with God, which is a form of prayer. I was taught never to question God, but I needed answers.

I fired off questions, crying, yelling, and asking God how He could do this to me. I had waited so long to get married only to have the husband He gave me stripped away. I was riddled with anger and guilt. Not just the guilt over not being able to save my husband, but survivor's guilt. Any time I laughed, smiled, or simply enjoyed life, guilt crept in and hit me so hard. I thought the tears would never end. I thought my life was over too.

I began questioning what was next. Who was going to keep the car maintained? Who was going to take out the garbage? How do I move on? I soon learned it's not about moving on, but moving forward. This is why we need a solid support system–good friends and people who are in our corner. My mother, who I affectionately call *Maggie*, knew all too well about losing a spouse because my father died in 2000. She was my rock and my everything as I struggled with adjusting to life as a widow.

My family (especially my eldest niece, female cousins, and aunties–biological and other) became my shoulders and sounding boards. My sorority sisters of Alpha Kappa Alpha Sorority, Incorporated® (especially Eta Omega Omega Chapter, "94 Plus", and my mentors) rallied around me (and continue to rally around me); helping with the funeral arrangements, slept over, came by daily, called, texted, and prayed. My manager and team at work gave me the space that I needed as well as hugs just because. My sisters and brothers in Christ at Unity Baptist Tabernacle, my home church, continuously lifted me in prayer and ministered to my soul with words of encouragement and through songs. My social media family: classmates from Mount Vernon High School and my alma mater, Morgan State University, loved on me in-person and online. Last but certainly not least, my friends–my "day ones" and sister-girls listened even when no words were being spoken.

All of the support was good, but I was still hurting, angry, depressed, and inconsolable. At the compassionate urging of my manager, I found a therapist through my company's employee assistance program who recommended a group therapy session with other women who also lost a spouse/partner. I went through the journey with those nine other women who really understood what I was going through. We bonded through our pain and maintain that bond till this day. By participating in individual and group therapy sessions, I learned that I could grieve in whatever way I needed to, and there was no timetable for it. Prior to that, I was grieving the way I thought everyone else wanted me to, ultimately doing a disservice to myself.

I let myself cry again and embraced the cleansing tears. Social media become my online journal, and I received massive support, even from those I considered acquaintances. One of my posts caught the attention of someone who not only recommended a personal development workshop offered by Momentum Education, but paid for it. I was already making strides to move forward, but Momentum catapulted me into an entirely different stratosphere. I discovered myself again. The weight of the guilt I felt slowly melted away, and I felt lighter. I'd gone back to church, but out of obligation to appease my mother. Now I was finally able to go to service, enjoy it and really hear from God. My anger dissipated as He whispered to me that Neil really was at peace. God gave my beloved the peace he needed, even if it meant leaving me.

I talk to Neil often and stopped waiting for him to appear to me in a dream as so many others mentioned happened to them. I got a dog and named him NeMo: "Ne" for Neil and "Mo" for Monica so that #TeamNeMo could live on. NeMo is a Godsend, and I believe Neil instructs the pooch when to sit on my lap, lick my face or look at me with those cute, big brown eyes. I find comfort in this heartfelt belief.

People always told me I was strong, but I needed to see and experience that strength for myself. September 2018, I went back to school for my MBA. I graduated in May 2021 with Distinction with a dual concentration in Accounting and Finance. I'm proud of my accomplishment because, by the grace of God, I pushed through sadness, loneliness, and heartache to accomplish my goal. I smile, laugh, and enjoy life knowing that Neil–my Snoopy, is smiling, laughing, and enjoying everything with me, his Hunnie Bunnie, from Heaven. Trust me when I say I miss my husband every day, and he'll always be the love of my life, but I'm at peace now. I've even started dating and laughingly believe I had to kiss some toads before Neil approved my next suitor.

I'm still a work in progress and ride the waves of grief when I have one of those days, but I don't ride them alone. I faithfully use my support system. While my conversations with God are more loving and pleasant these days, I still have moments where I ask questions, and I'm okay with that. I know that it's only because of God that I didn't lose myself or my sanity. I'm still standing, and I recognize that I am stronger. I also recognize that there IS life after death.

Becoming Quanda

QUANDA DULIN

My mother named me Quanda, after a cute little girl she met while riding in a taxi when she was seven months pregnant with me. By some accounts, Quanda means "Queen," but if I'm honest with myself, I didn't always see the name as befitting for me. I was born in the early 70s, on the tail end of the civil rights movement, when Black people were slightly woke in some areas, but not enough in others. I wasn't light-skinned with soft flowing hair and almond-shaped eyes. I didn't have thin lips with a defined nose indicative of someone who was akin to Caucasian or indigenous people. By society's standards, I wasn't the cute little girl my mother saw me as. Consequently, I had a complex growing up in this era. I recall being a little girl who constantly wondered why God brought me here; my mind swirled with curiosity about my purpose, intention, and being.

My mother was the center of my universe; she was born to give. She bathed me, made sure I ate and had clothes, and taught me songs. She made sure all of my needs were met. In fact, the earliest memories I have of my mother is her preoccupation with the needs of others. She was the neighborhood mother whom everyone loved. Her front door was always open to visitors, and she never met a stranger. In the middle of our kitchen was a round table where young people sat to discuss difficult decisions about dating, relationships, family matters, etc. They disclosed their most personal information at that table, expressing guilt, fear, love, hate, and other emotions. My mother provided informal counseling to anyone who walked through her door and needed an ear to listen. Yet, as her daughter, I've always felt a bit disconnected from her. Mainly because I wanted her to utilize some of the advice she dispensed to others to escape from the abusive relationship she'd been in since she was twenty-one years old. A relationship that was not only detrimental to her, but adversely impacted the lives and well-being of her children.

One hot summer day, I was in my parents' bedroom, awakening from a nap. Laying quietly in my crib, unable to speak, I waited for someone to come to get me as I watched the sun pierce through the dark green roller shades. I peered across the room and spotted my biological father, Bill, sleeping. Bill was an evil man who didn't even like himself. I tried laying as still as I could, wanting attention, but Bill's kind of attention wasn't what I needed.

Hearing the faint sound of my mother downstairs entertaining friends, I cried out so she would come to get me. She couldn't hear me, so I cried louder and louder. Finally, Bill jumped out of bed, looked me square in the eyes, and cursed me out. Stifled by fear, I went silent for a moment before screaming uncontrollably.

Annoyed by my sobs, Bill jumped out of bed again, shouting for me to shut up. Not yet even a year old, I wanted Bill to feel the disdain I had for him. But what my tiny mouth uttered was unintelligible.

Unfortunately, Bill's personality was consistent; he didn't spare any of us. At age 3, I watched him beat my mother for nothing and terrorize my little brother. That evening, I witnessed him throw my 8-month-old brother from across the room into his crib. Cautiously, my mother slowly approached him and said, "Bill, don't worry. I'll take care of him." In response, Bill turned around, knocked her down, and began kicking her.

Bill beat my mother from her room to my room. I tried to hand her the fan to defend herself, but she was too distracted to grab it. Finally, I screamed at the top of my lungs, "I hate you!" For a quick second, Bill glared at me with cold eyes, mentally banishing me back to the infant in the crib filled with utter disdain for him. Without a word, he continued assaulting my mother. This was one of the countless times that I watched him physically and mentally abuse her. I wanted so badly for her to leave him, but she wouldn't.

According to Bill, his mother abandoned him when he was an infant; he never referred to her as anything other than vile names. I sat with her before she died, and she told me that she had him when she was 14 years old—his father was 21. His father's parents immediately fell in love with Bill and took him straight home from the hospital to help her out. He was born prematurely, so they turned a dresser drawer into a bed and provided him with what they could at the time, allowing Bill's mother to drop by to see him from time to time. Eventually, Bill's grandparents told her that they would take care of him, and she didn't have to come by anymore. After all, his mother was still climbing trees and having fun as a teen. So, she respected their wishes and didn't return. She moved to New York, and Bill has hated her ever since.

Bill's perception of his mother and her reasons for leaving were totally different than what really happened. As a result of what he thinks his mother did, I believe he hated all women. His unrestrained hate towards my mother and indifference towards me was proof. If only he understood that his teenage mother didn't have the intellectual, financial, or emotional capacity to provide him with what he needed at the time, things might have been different. She told me her mother left her with her grandmother too. So, she felt she did the best she could by allowing his grandparents to give him the love and support he needed.

I was invisible to Bill. He worked for the New York Department of Transportation, the first real job he obtained shortly after I was born. Since he typically worked from 11:00 p.m. to 7:00 a.m., I didn't see him much. I don't believe he cared to be seen, either. During the week, he listened to baseball and slept, but on Friday nights, Bill emerged as a socialite. This was payday, so my younger brother and I counted on coming home to a house full of men and loud, loose women scattered about the living room and huddled around the dining room table nursing Bacardi and Coke and cocaine.

Their conversations were littered with lewd jokes objectifying women and romanticized how much the men didn't care about anything and anyone. They boldly talked about their plans to

score more drugs and women. Our young ears overheard it all—
no details were spared. At five and eight years old, respectively,
my brother and I weren't psychologically safe to be introduced to
"Bill, the legend." However, we desperately wanted to know our
father, but as kids, we had nothing to offer him.

One night, my younger brother broke out in hives as he sat
nervously at the top stairs, peeking through the banister to catch
a glimpse of what was happening. I walked past him, reminding
him to take his medication. As I retreated back to my bedroom,
I fantasized about having my own family one day. I brushed my
hair, imagining it was long and soft as I dreamt of the kind of
wife I'd be to Michael Jackson. Searching every angle of myself,
I struggled to find something I liked about myself. Sadly, I drew
a blank.

Every now and then, I went to the top of the stairs to see
what was going on. The smell of Pall Mall cigarettes, Bacardi and
Odyssey, Avon perfume, and hints of marijuana permeated the air.
I strolled into my mother's room, opened her bottle of Jeanate'
and sniffed, hoping to drown out the other intrusive odors. It was
also a comforting reminder that Mommy would be home soon.

My three older brothers' lifestyle choices closely mimicked
that of my father. I was jealous of them because at least they
had a connection to him. I, on the other hand, was scared and
lonely. Mommy was there, but she had a lot on her plate—with Bill
occupying most of that space. To escape, I often imagined living
somewhere else or dreaming what our lives would be like once Bill
died from the emphysema he'd been diagnosed with.

While Bill made me feel invisible, boys my age began taking notice to me. Once I hit fourth grade, I became aware of my growing curves and the boys fascination with me. My womanly body attracted attention the other girls didn't get. At 12-years-old, I met a gorgeous guy named Unique. Unique smelled good and called me *cutie*, which was enough for me. When he asked how old I was, I lied and said I was sixteen. From there, we talked on the phone until Unique invited me to his home in Cambria Heights, and I gingerly accepted the invite. I threw on my Hawaiian shorts with a matching top, a pair of sneakers, slicked my hair into the tightest ponytail and made the 20-block hike to Cambria Heights, where he lived.

As soon as I got to Unique's house, we immediately began to kiss. I felt as though my body was exploding from the inside out, and I could barely stand it. He did things I had no business doing at my age, but it felt right since we kept our clothes on. When we were finished, neither one of us said a word. I walked back home, took a shower, and went to bed as though nothing ever happened. I didn't even understand the seriousness of the predicament I placed myself in.

Unique didn't force me to take my clothes off, and I didn't have to. But our encounter provoked me to chase that feeling I got with him. All I thought about was sex. I wanted to be noticed and loved like Blake loved Crystal on *Dynasty*, Luke loved Laura on *General Hospital* or Jonathan loved Jennifer on *Hart to Hart*. Those were my examples of what it meant to be in a relationship, mixed with a little Roxanne Shante.

On my mission to be loved, I began dating a boy in Cambria Heights. He was no more than two years older than me and had recently survived an accident, rendering him with limited mobility. I walked to his house and spent time with him while I plotted my next move. Unexpectedly, I met an older woman who took an interest in me and disrupted the plans I had to have sex with this boy and marry him. After I confided in her, she gently educated me about life and occupied my time by taking me to the ballet and teaching me how to cook, clean, and iron. She helped me experience things I wasn't used to and focused all of her time on me. The more attention she gave me, the more my desire to have sex slowly dissipated.

One day at 13, I was lying in my brother's room on my stomach when I heard someone coming up the stairs. It turned out to be a 23-year-old family friend who was visiting. He came in the room, laid on top of me, and took advantage of my limited ability to move—pinning me down as I fought back ferociously. I felt myself becoming angry at my body; I didn't want to do what he was trying to force me to, so I struggled to get him off of me. Finally, I got from under him and ran out of the room.

I discussed the incident with the older woman whom I befriended, and she encouraged me to tell my mother about the incident. I told my mother, and she said she confronted him…but nothing changed. He was still allowed to come to the house. In fact, the next time we were alone, he taunted me, saying, "Maybe the next time we can finish, and you won't tell." I was enraged. I felt like the helpless infant in the crib again.

Before long, I was full-fledged teen attending high school. I adapted to high school quite well. I had a boyfriend who was the sweetest guy. Walking to the bus stop, we held hands; he carried my book bag, walked me to my classes, and called me *Boo*. Best of all, we weren't sexually active. The problem was, I always found something wrong with him. I complained about everything he did until his parents intervened and ended our relationship.

In my third year of high school, I met "Les." Les was tall, handsome, and extremely intelligent. He came to my house every day and watched my family interactions without uttering a word. I recall my aunt Erla saying, "That boy is going to ruin Quanda, I can see the handwriting on the wall." When my mother told me what my aunt said, I angrily spat, "She's crazy!"

Les could dance, and I loved how he spoke French in my ear. We would sneak to the Village in Manhattan, which was a big deal for me because it never occurred to me that I could take the train without my mother's permission. Les questioned my obedience to my mother. He pushed her limits and encouraged me to lie to her. I foolishly thought he was so "amazing" and that I was in "love."

Eventually, Les and I began having sex every day. It was like he was obsessed with me. At first, I was flattered, but after a while, our encounters became annoying and downright painful to the point where I didn't want to have sex anymore. I tried to set boundaries, but Les saw it as rejection.

The first time I expressed my discomfort and made him stop, Les beat me like I was a man. For the next year, he beat me for everything he perceived to be an insult to his ego. I got pregnant and aborted the baby and even contracted an STD from Les, which he denied giving to me despite him being the only person I'd been with. He was so angry, he slandered my name and tried to destroy me.

By the time I enrolled in Norfolk State University, I was broken. I lost my sense of self and longed to disappear. As the other students on campus had fun, dated, partied, and participated in collegiate activities, I was withdrawn. I barely functioned and didn't care anymore. At least I had my roommate, who attended high school with me. She is probably one of the realest chicks I have ever known. I'm grateful that she held me down through my darkest days and never wavered. She had my back when Les followed me to Norfolk State and stalked me. Word of the ordeal quickly spread, and I was humiliated on top of everything else. But when things finally ended with Les, I started dating Darren.

At first, I struggled to connect with Darren. After all the trauma I experienced at the hands of men, I felt like they were nothing–him included. But Darren stuck by me, loved me unconditionally, and provided financial assistance for my college education. Darren taught me how to love again. The way he loved me, made me want to love myself. For the first time in my life, I felt beautiful. He took me on trips, taught me about business and the importance of having multiple streams of income, loved and nurtured my soul, and served as my twin flame.

Tragically, on June 13, 2010, Darren was killed by a drunk driver. My whole world stopped. Before he died, Darren helped my mother put me through undergrad and graduate school, encouraged me to get licensed as an advanced practitioner, accepted my son as his own, encouraged me to apply for a government job as a licensed clinical therapist, and provided me with the necessary steps to start a business. Darren believed in me. His actions taught me what love is and what it is not. I loved that man. I didn't fully understand the meaning of love, but I certainly do now, thanks to him.

The birth of my first child also taught me love I'd never known. I gave birth to a precious baby boy, at 26, while I was still in school. I knew I wouldn't be able to pursue my degree and devote the time I needed to be the best mother to my son, so my mother encouraged me to bring him home. That was the best decision I could have ever made. My healing from the tumultuous relationship with my father arrived through my son. My mother always held me down, but my father was never actively involved in any of his children's lives, so I learned to manage my expectations of him from the time I was a baby. However, he took great care of my little one, and it was admirable. He and my mother made sure all my son's needs were met. I recall him putting my son in his umbrella stroller, taking him to daycare, giving him fruit snacks to reward good behavior, teaching him how to feed his pet birds, allowing him to take naps with him, singing *Blues Clues*, bathing him, helping him with his homework and watching baseball games with him.

I watched as my father held my son's hand as they walked to the store, how he hugged and kissed him and made certain he was clothed, bathed, fed, and most of all loved. Through this experience, I was able to feel compassion and forgive a man who never asked for my forgiveness. My father's relationship with his grandson helped me understand that hurt people do indeed hurt people. This was the beginning of my restoration. I was willing to embrace my father for who he was and began loving myself without the need for validation from him, which quickly expanded to other people in my life, particularly men. I began to stand in self-love.

Through God's abounding grace, I continue to recover from my past wounds. I have learned that nothing can happen unless God allows it to happen. In my darkest hours, I have learned to depend on HIM as my source. Many friends have come and gone; there have been men who have proclaimed love and one who has actually demonstrated love; however, God loves me best. He placed me in a home where my father didn't know how to love me, and my mother was a survivor of domestic violence. I witnessed this with my heart, eyes, and ears.

Seemingly, it was all a part of His plan. The trauma I experienced as a child led me into the field of mental health. With my mother serving as an example, I realized that helping others get through emotional pain and trauma is what wounded healers do. So, when a child comes to my office to receive services because they have witnessed abuse, I got them. God allowed me to witness my father's substance abuse and experience its impact on my life by feeling his absence. What He taught me is that His presence is bigger. Now when I encounter a person who is struggling with co-dependence, I empathize with their pain. God allowed me to experience domestic violence, the shame of being impregnated at 15, having an abortion, and contracting an STD to help someone other than myself. I have a clear understanding and am non-judgmental of men and women with similar difficult situations and decisions to make.

God provided me with a father who served in the Army, fought in the Korean War, and returned home with Post-Traumatic Stress Disorder (PTSD). I am now the Director of the Vet Center, a government agency that was developed by Vietnam veterans for men and women in the service returning from war in need of readjustment counseling to assist with the transition from military to civilian life. We also provide counseling to survivors of sexual trauma experienced while in the military. He allowed me to experience not feeling loved by my own father, often seeking love and affection from men. Now I pour love into my children, ensuring that they never question my love and don't feel the need to seek it elsewhere. The icing on top is that I've been able to get a glimpse of the table He prepared for me, in the presence of people who did not know who I was becoming.

The Makings of a Mother

SHANISHA COLLINS

"What if I just jump?" Somehow, asking myself that question from my mother's 20th-floor apartment didn't seem unreasonable. I was broken, lonely, scared, and thought I was losing my mind, so why not jump? I had nothing to live for anyway, right? If life had meaning, I couldn't see it. I no longer wanted to be a mother or somebody's daughter. Friends didn't matter, not that they were real, anyway. I sank into a place where I was simply existing…and I didn't want to exist anymore.

For some strange reason, I found myself comforted by the thought of death, with very little reason not to act on impulse. "Just end it all," I tried convincing myself. "Go ahead, end the pain."

…so I jumped.

I jumped right in my car and drove myself to the hospital. I laid in the sterile bed for days, trying to wrap my head around the fact that I, Shanisha Collins, had a mental breakdown. How could that be possible? I was supposed to be the strong one. No matter the circumstance, I was the one who was supposed to be able to withstand it all.

After leaving what I thought was my dream job, I had spent the previous eighteen months building a consulting firm. One night, I was jolted from my sleep, dreaming about my business. I jumped up, gathered my notebooks, and started sorting through them. As I flipped through the pages, it hit me: everything I needed to get started was right in front of me. A rush of excitement came over me, which turned into a two-week experience that I still can't fully comprehend. All I know is I dove in headfirst and didn't sleep or eat for two weeks as I worked to put the pieces together. Everything seemed so clear to me, until one day, it wasn't.

My breakdown came early in 2019. I spent a Saturday morning at a cousin's birthday party and had plans to go shopping with my mother and daughter later that afternoon. Before going on our shopping excursion, we stopped by my mother's apartment, when I was suddenly slammed with intense, suffocating despair. My mind started racing, and I was immediately overwhelmed to the point where I wanted to die. Fear gripped every part of me; the last thing I wanted to do was live.

I immediately went to the hospital, where I explained what I was feeling and was told I was experiencing a manic episode. Doctors quickly diagnosed me as bipolar, and I spent three days in the hospital. Since that time, I've seen countless therapists and tried various drugs as a result of being diagnosed and misdiagnosed with a variety of issues. It took a year and a half of advocating for myself to locate the right therapist who finally diagnosed me correctly: I was suffering from Post-Traumatic Stress Disorder (PTSD) and Obsessive-Compulsive Disorder (OCD). Although no one wants to receive that type of news, I was relieved to finally know what was wrong with me. Trying to find help when you've fallen into the pit of despair is frustrating; knowing when to get the help you need takes courage.

Prior to the manic episode, I had knee surgery and spent months in the house, causing me to fall apart slowly but surely. Who knew the solitude I was craving would manifest into a mental breakdown? The reality is, my issues were there before I tumbled down the hill that messed up my knee in the first place. But I stayed too busy to slow down and deal with them. Sitting in the house doing nothing for an extended time and being unable to walk forced me to confront all the things I'd avoided facing before.

Traumatic memories from my childhood, young adulthood, and my failed marriage plagued my mind. Grasping for a way to breathe through the nightmares, I had to admit to myself that years prior to my breakdown, I'd received several warnings that it was coming. My trusted advisors, family, and friends saw the train wreck approaching and advised me to slow down. I was tired and knew I needed a break, but I literally didn't know how to take one. Several people depended on me whom I didn't want to let down, so I kept pushing because pushing was all I knew to do. I didn't know I was pressed beyond my limits and never imagined how it would come crashing down and affect the way I parented my children.

I absolutely adore my children, whom I affectionately refer to as the B&G. "B" is for boy, or my son, Kalear; "G" is my girl, my daughter, Jeshani. My poor kids. They've gone through everything with me, both good and bad. Why couldn't I foresee how pushing myself through trauma without proper healing would affect them so badly?

As a single mother, I've always felt the weight of balancing the line between being both disciplinarian and nurturer, but somewhere, the balance got off. I grew up in a strict military household, run on strict discipline and order, and felt like I was in the army myself. Somehow, I found myself implementing the same spirit-breaking tactics from my childhood to raise my children, with the intention of building them back up later. I figured if the rigid discipline and order made me a better person, it would do the same for my children. But it had adverse effects on them and left me feeling like the worst mother ever.

Have you ever blamed yourself for your children's behavior, like you haven't done enough to prevent it? Taking accountability as if you were directly responsible because of your own behavior? I was seriously angry with myself because I felt like I'd failed my kids. Maybe I didn't praise them enough or do my best to build up their self-confidence. Maybe I was too tough on them, only paying attention to their mistakes and ignoring their triumphs. Maybe I just didn't love them enough. For too long, I allowed the enemy to fill my head with all of these negative thoughts.

Now I realize I was taking things too personally. In my mind, I had to be a perfect mother who raised perfect children, which meant when they made a mistake, I came down hard on them.

To me, their errors represented me and my parenting, and I wasn't having it. The world isn't forgiving, so I was determined to prepare them to avoid any issues that would count as a strike against them. At least that's what I thought I was doing. In reality, I was parenting out of fear instead of love.

Don't get me wrong, I love my kids more than anything. But I often found it challenging to strike a fair balance between disciplinarian and nurturer, which created an environment where at times they didn't feel like they were enough or didn't have the opportunity to learn from their mistakes. Their need to meet my standard of perfection often crippled them because they feared making mistakes, which at times, prevented them from moving forward and taking risks needed to be successful.

I know I haven't always been the best parent, but now I'm trying my best to do all of the things I should've done when my children were younger. Sometimes I feel like I'm running out of time because they're almost grown, but I'm optimistic that they'll be able to heal from the mistakes I've made as a parent. I thought my breakdown was the worst thing that could ever happen to me. The mere shame of it caused me to hide it from people, but my breakdown forced me to acknowledge my trauma and begin to heal. Today, I'm working overtime to correct my parenting mistakes, so my kids won't be forced to carry their traumatic childhood into their adult lives.

My kids are really wonderful. They are two of the most respectful, loving, accepting, and funniest people ever. Kalear is a history lover and hopes to be a historian. Jeshani is a serial entrepreneur who has launched several businesses and dreams of continuing down the path of entrepreneurship. Both of them are absolutely destined for greatness in the future.

The pressure of raising a young Black man and woman is heavy. My fear for their Black lives and the unrealistic expectations of perfection turned me into an overbearing mom. But our journey hasn't been all bad. I've always reassured my children they can talk to me about anything; no subject's taboo in our household, so they take full advantage of the opportunity to be transparent, even when it involves me. We've traveled the country and connected with an amazing group of mothers who love traveling with their children as well. We're well aware of social issues which affect our community, and our kids are well-versed in how to advocate for themselves and others. We've attended countless social justice rallies, the 50th anniversary of The March on Washington, the 50th anniversary of Freedom Summer, and most recently participated in a feature for the 100th anniversary of the Tulsa Race Massacre.

The realization that my unhealed trauma has caused my children pain is too much to bear at times. I've shamed myself for feeling inadequate; however, I am thankful to have an opportunity to right my wrongs. Each time I wake up, I'm able to make a conscious decision to be the nurturer my children need me to be, and on the days I fall short, I know I can start over again. There's no need to wait until tomorrow; I'm learning to hit the reset button daily and to be okay with making mistakes. I've learned to show my children that I'm not perfect, and neither are they. I'm learning to be more forgiving–starting with myself, and I'm doing all I can to make sure they don't follow down the same dark path as me. As a result, we're in therapy now, on the way to healing.

I pray my children will make themselves proud without seeking external approval and that they'll heal from the trauma in their lives. I pray they'll embrace their gifts and activate them to impact the world. I pray they know how amazing I really think they are and how much I truly love them. I pray they know they are more than enough and are deserving of the greatness awaiting them. I pray they know mistakes are a part of life and that perfection isn't real. Most of all, I pray my children are able to forgive me.

When we know better, we do better, but we still have to deal with the issues we create in the meantime. Mistakes will be made. Frustration will build. Tears will flow. Through it all, I've learned that mothering is hard. Mothering while trying to be perfect and unhealed can be detrimental. During this healing process, I'm learning to embrace my imperfections and not allow my past mistakes to define me or determine my children's future. Every day is an opportunity to break the cycle and start anew. Beginning NOW.

7 Years of Luck

SHAREMA HARVELL

"Luck is when preparation meets opportunity." I remember hearing this statement and thinking I must have always been in preparation. I am Sharema Harvell, mother of four: three on earth, one in Heaven. My daughter Sydney is 21, my daughter Taylor is 14, and my son Jermel Jr. (JJ) is 10. My son Sean Marvell Ricks, who is eternally 12 years, 11 months, and three weeks old, would've been 19 years old this year. I am an author, comedian, business advisor, radio show host and producer, seminar host, television host, community leader, peer/youth mentor, and a walking testimony.

I currently go by the name *Rema The Great*. I chose that name because I am the greatest person I know. I wasn't always the greatest, though. I was once the most manipulative, conniving, arrogant, conceited, and possibly the most intolerable person anyone has ever met. Let me take you back in time a few years ago, seven, to be exact.

It was January, and I was enrolled in a back-to-work program to lift my welfare sanction due to me not reporting for a job program. The irony, right? I had a reputation for going back and forth to these programs, getting the sanction lifted, then slipping back into my old habits. This was my cycle.

At this point, I'd been an adult entertainer for seven years and a radio talk show host and producer for four years. I was also a heavy hitter in the underground BBW (Big Beautiful Woman) adult scene in NYC. I'd hosted a few local events and interviewed the majority of talent in the urban adult industry on one of the shows I produced, *Outta Da Box Radio*. When the show went off the air in 2013, a friend asked what I wanted to do.

"I want to interview people on television about their relationships," I replied.

"Well, you're going to have to go to school for that," he advised.

"Oh no, I don't," I said matter of factly. "I know how to read a dictionary, and I know how to use a calculator. I don't have to go to school!" I knew what I wanted, but life had a whole different plan for me.

Okay, back to the story…

So, I was sitting in this welfare program where I met another participant. I don't remember her name, but she was a graduate of the College of New Rochelle. She told a few other participants and me about the school and why we should enroll, but I already had a few reasons for not going. For one thing, my mother and grandmother graduated from there. To me, they were ignorant, so I wouldn't gain anything from any school they attended. Secondly, the school's campus was way out in the Bronx, and I needed to be closer to Harlem. I didn't want to commute, not even to the Bronx. Although the woman made a compelling argument, I hadn't been in school in over a decade and had no plans of going back. Period. Or so I thought.

One day, I was spring cleaning, and my cousin and I were going through a bunch of old papers when I stumbled across a postcard that said **The College of New Rochelle. New Location, The Rosa Parks Harlem Campus**. I instantly teared up and said, "Okay, God, I'll go." How did I know God was talking to me? That postcard didn't even have my address printed on it, yet I received it. No one can tell me that wasn't God working.

A week later, I was enrolled as a psychology major. It was both the scariest and best thing I could've ever done in my life. Back then, I didn't understand why I chose my major, but I sure know now. I'm interested in getting into people's heads and understanding why they behave the way they do. Coming from a background like mine, I was especially curious about how low self-esteem could help people make money more than being confident.

Although I was now a college student, I remained an adult entertainer. I loved it. The attention, the manipulation, the idea of being able to dress up and get paid to be a fantasy was all a girl could want. Men went crazy over me, women looked up to me, and I ran New York City like my name was Diddy. It was the life! But in life, there are challenges.

During my third semester, I received a letter from the housing office saying that I had to pay $1200 in back rent in less than two weeks or I'd be evicted immediately. I was devastated. Up until this point, I never considered escorting; I just wasn't interested and didn't know how to do it anyway. I'd observed some female escorts and even tried it a time or two, but not steadily. However, this letter told me it was time to go on the stroll. As I mentioned, I was no spring chicken. After seven years of watching others do it and fail, you learn how to win. I contacted a close friend of mine and asked, "How do I sell my P@#%&?"

"How much are you thinking?" he casually responded like I was asking for interview tips.

"$300 an hour, $150 for a half, and $100 for a quickie," I told him, feeling as if I was worth at least that much.

"Look at it like this," he said. "If you sold it for $50 per person and service two people a day, that would be $700 a week, $2800 a month, and $36,400 a year. While you're waiting for a person to pay the amount you're asking, another girl is banking on $50 a person."

His advice made sense, but I was set on what I wanted. "Nope, I'll sell it for $300," I insisted.

If the clients wanted me, then that's what they were going to have to pay. Sticking to my guns, I learned how to post online, so the neighborhood pimps where I was doing in-calls wouldn't harass or run me out of town. I posted my services on a well-known website and looked for areas where no other women looked like me. I refused to change my price as long as I was in NYC because changing the price opens the door for negotiation and shows desperation. Compromise meant anyone could talk you down on your price, so I came up with my own rules to work by:

Rule #1: It's my body, I make the rules.

Rule #2: Don't meet new clients after midnight.

Rule #3: Have a quota—my quota was $600 a night.

Rule #4: Let the client pay for the room if it's an outcall.

Rule #5: Never work with another woman.

These were the laws I lived by. I learned the hard way with each one and had to figure them out quickly. I learned how to make bank by talking live on camera for five hours every other night, collect my coins, tips, and cash out. I also performed private shows via video chat, using my cell phone to film my sessions and edit the footage for resale on various websites.

Escorting and radio afforded me the opportunity to travel all over the nation. I was asked to host events out of town and negotiated with the promoter to either get round trip transportation or lodging for 2-4 days. This way, I could make my money back. Between 2014 and 2015, I hosted adult events in Las Vegas, Memphis, Detroit, Atlanta, Miami, Baltimore, and of course, throughout New York. Also, in the fall of 2014, I responded to an online ad searching for a co-host for a radio talk show and got the job. I loved the opportunity because I got to work alongside the owner of the station. As a personality, I'd always wanted to run my own station, so this was perfect. I escorted and co-hosted the talk show, making money by doing what I was passionate about while attending school and making appearances at local adult parties.

In the summer of 2015, I was afforded the opportunity to learn the engineering boards and how to run the station. Our regular DJ and engineer had been given the opportunity for more gigs, which was great for her but bad for our show. The host had to engineer the program, which made me the face of the show. I hated it and told him to teach me how to engineer. Over the next three months, I learned how to run the station, messing up at least 30 shows before getting it right. Shortly after I learned what I was doing, he trusted me to run the station, and I was given the keys to an office off of Times Square. I was ecstatic, but I didn't want to stop there. I told him I wanted my own talk show, and he said I could have it if I did it live by myself. I agreed, and shortly after, *The Big Skweeze* show debuted. There I was, a powerhouse, running a radio station and working towards my BA, still bringing in money from escorting, live camming, and hosting events. Life was good, but not for long.

I remember November 6, 2015, like yesterday. My youngest daughter Taylor came into my room, requesting to speak to her father or grandmother. I called both of them, but neither answered.

"It's okay, Hun. They love you, they're just busy right now," I told her. Instantly her face went blank. "Taylor, what's the matter?"

"I can't tell you," she said…right before passing out. When she hit the floor, I was in shock. I quickly pulled myself together, then called 911. On the way to the hospital, I called my children's father. He was so nonchalant about our daughter being rushed to the emergency room; I wanted to hang up in his face. After being seen, the doctors said Taylor passed out because she hadn't eaten lunch earlier at school. A few years later, we discovered she experiences syncope– the temporary loss of consciousness caused by a decrease in blood pressure.

When we left the hospital, Taylor went to her maternal grandmother's house while I returned home and sat with my son Sean in his room. Since I was upset with his father, I said, "This year you can spend your birthday with whoever you want, you don't have to spend it with your dad. He'll call, but you can choose where you want to be."

"So, you don't want me to answer when my dad calls?" he asked.

Conflicted, I heard myself say, "You can do what you want."

The next day, Sean was so worried about Taylor that he asked if he could go to their grandmother's to be with her, and I agreed. When they returned Sunday night, they were both having issues with their asthma, but I only had one machine. "Mom, let Taylor get on first," Sean told me. "I'll be okay." From what I was told, he'd been nursing her asthma all that day. By the time Taylor finished treatment, and it was time for him to get on the machine, Sean was too far gone. All I remember him saying was, "Mom, please call 911! It's not working." Within five minutes, my son went from normal to passed out in my arms. He died before the ambulance got to us. My life would never be the same again.

Sean died November 8, 2015; his birthdate is November 14th–his funeral was held November 16th. That entire week, I was held up and carried by my son's spirit and God himself. I can remember feeling a divine touch, like from a prophet or the Holy Spirit. I spoke to people and gave them readings about their life that were so impactful, they'd cry. I also called on God, and He performed miracles within moments.

The first miracle I recall was having a Verizon bill that was over $700. The notice said that if I didn't pay at least $500 by December 23rd, the cable would be disconnected. By then, I'd quit escorting and adult entertainment; I didn't want Sean seeing me doing those things from Heaven. Quitting left me with no real income, so as I read the bill, I opened my mouth and started talking to God.

"God, these kids been through so much. I need YOU to take care of this bill. I don't have the money, and I'm not going back to who I was just to pay it."

On December 23rd, the internet was cut off. By December 24th, it was back on, with a notice in my email which read: **Please wait while we reconnect your service.** Not one person had my cable information, no one. On December 26th, I received a bill in the mail that was one sheet thick. Now let's be real, when have you ever seen a bill that was only one sheet thick? Never. The bill said I had to pay $500 by January 3rd, or my cable would be turned off. God granted me another two weeks to pay that bill! I used every dime I had to get it paid.

The second miracle came one day when I didn't have any food in the cabinet; however, all of my son's friends constantly wanted to visit and stay over. They kept coming, but I didn't have anything to feed them. "God, You are all mighty," I said, "I don't have any food to feed these kids. I need food. Matter of fact, I need so much food, I want there to be fruit flies by the time You're done." A week later, I received an open welfare case, plus an open food stamp case at the same time. I received over $500 monthly in stamps, where I was only supposed to receive $300.

By the time I moved that August, I still had fruit flies; however, I feared this newfound attention from God, so I ran from it.

From that December until May of 2016, I worked to finish my semester in school, then took a two-semester break, along with a five-month leave from work so I could get myself and my children together. I placed my eldest in ACS custody because I couldn't console her and my younger children while trying to keep myself together, too. As bad as it was, my life was about to get much worse. I wasn't ready for what happened next.

That spring, I started using drugs. I don't remember how it started, but the drugs helped me deal with everything and forget what I was going through. I finally felt free. At first, I was using sporadically until I was able to indulge more regularly. Eventually, I was referred to a dealer in my neighborhood. I'd bought from him before via a close friend of mine but hadn't met him before. Even still, I trusted his product. When I met him, he turned out to be an older guy who looked unkempt and wasn't anyone I'd dare attempt to talk to. However, I was lonely, and he was available, so I did what I wanted to do—I began an affair with my drug dealer.

I became addicted to molly very easily. It was my comfort. What made it so easy was that I felt so alone even though I had lots of family and friends. I was lost and felt like I couldn't share my thoughts with people without them feeling sorry for me or assuming they had to watch what they said in front of me. I hated feeling like a sad case, so I avoided everyone. I locked myself in my room all day, binging on molly almost every day for months. That's when God visited me, changing my life forever yet again.

It was a regular day, and the drugs dehydrated me; however, I wasn't paying attention to my body, especially the pain on my lower left side that I brushed off and treated with some irritable bowel medication and a pain killer. I waited a few hours, then took a shot of alcohol; a half-hour later, I took some molly. I sat on the bed waiting for my dealer to come by, when suddenly my head was burning. It wasn't like a fever burn, but more like the inside of my head got warm, and my body followed. I hopped in the shower, but not even the cold water cooled me down. With no other recourse, I took a shot of Tylenol, got dressed, and dialed 911.

I swear if I hadn't taken the Tylenol, I may have fully overdosed. I'd never experienced anything like that in my entire life and was terrified. I was rushed to the hospital, thankful to be conscious. By the time I got there, the burning sensation had decreased, I was put on an IV and told I was dehydrated, but I knew better—I'd almost died. Facing death should've been enough for me to stop, but it wasn't. Two weeks later, I tried it again and thought I was dying, but it was an anxiety attack. Thank God I'm still here to share my testimony.

Over the next few months, I got off molly cold turkey. But life threw other curveballs my way. Because I'd been so dangerously reckless sexually, I caught syphilis–which was ironic, considering I'd never contracted an STD when I was escorting. I was also battling severe migraines, grief, loneliness, confusion, hypochondria, anxiety, and panic disorder. I was completely jacked up.

The anxiety attacks sent me to the emergency room every few days, so much that it wasn't until hospital staff asked me who was at home with my kids and threatened to call ACS that I knew I had to figure something out. Although my cousin (their babysitter) was in her late twenties, medical personnel was alarmed by how frequently I visited the emergency room. I was put on Prozac; however, I thought the migraines were because of the Prozac, so I discontinued using it, going cold turkey yet again. This time I promised myself I'd figure it out, and that's just what I did.

Between 2017 and 2018, I started therapy, determined to identify the triggers behind my self-destructive behavior. I slowly started eliminating things out of my life and quit drinking, smoking cigarettes, and weed. Actually, I stopped everything just to see if that worked, and boy did it. The following year, during my last semester of school, I made the decision to work on myself more intensely. I was blessed to be introduced to a transformational personal development workshop. The first night I went, I was surprised how many people of color were happily participating. It weirded me out, but at the same time, I was intrigued. After signing up and completing four days of self-awareness and accepting who I was and who I no longer wanted to be, I decided I was going to be the best student I'd never been before, with renewed focus.

I took five courses, four of which were in psychology, receiving three A's and two B's. Overall, I graduated with a 2.9 GPA, and I was proud of myself. Out of all five years, it was the only semester I'd ever received an A. Convinced I could do it again, I promised myself that the next time I enroll in school, I'll get all A's, each and every time.

In August 2019, I enrolled in a 90-day leadership program with the same personal development community. I was the best

I'd ever been. I was able to look back to see how far I'd come and was able to see how far I wanted to go in the future. By the end of the leadership program, I had two new opportunities on the table. One was to join my neighborhood community team, and the second was to perform stand-up. I chose both.

To think, four years after having my world rocked following my son's passing, I had a team of people who believed in me, a strong support system, my children and I were healing, and I was able to process the idea of new beginnings. I even won a pitch contest! Long story short, while at a neighborhood event, I pitched an idea for a youth program to bridge the gap between youth and the entrepreneurs from my development. After all the votes were cast, my idea won. Because it was my winning season, I was also getting booked for comedy shows. After a while, I wasn't going to open mic events, I was hosting them. I was completely recharged!

Once COVID took over the world, I stopped doing stand-up and went out into the community, delivering food three times a week to disabled individuals and seniors. I didn't care about a check; I just wanted to help. Helping out introduced me to the many problems in my neighborhood I wasn't aware of in my fifteen years there. Prior to COVID, I never tried to get involved, but I am grateful I made the conscious effort to change that. By 2020, I'd become a known figure in my community. I assisted the mayor's office and city council with basic things like flyers and offered strategies for executing engagement and enrollment in programs that were needed in the community. For many years, I learned how to do so many different things, unaware when I'd need them. Who would've ever thought I learned all these skills to help my neighborhood?

One day while picking up flyers at a local organization, the director of the youth department asked if I would be interested in a position as a part-time youth mentor, which I gladly accepted. Prior to this offer, the last job I had was working at a fast-food restaurant back in 2018; I hadn't had a job on the books since. Up to this point, my only experience was in media, radio and production, and my degree was a Bachelor's in Psychology. For the past two years, I had questioned why God sent me to school for psychology. But on that day, I realized He was planting me in the field of social work.

I got the job, which I didn't think was possible because of my past and who I was. However, I realized it was because of my past and who I was that made me the right candidate for the job. Seemingly overnight, I went from being a part-time youth mentor, to being a full-time, salaried group facilitator for the *Alternative to Incarceration* program–where I motivate, empower, encourage and teach a special group of men who are all awaiting court dates. We perform community work together, share our testimonies, and allow ourselves to heal and help each other heal. While I'm doing what I love, I'm showing them how to fall in love with and be proud of themselves. I make it my business to teach them self-love and treat them like humans, not like their sentence as so many others do. I'm still being prepared and learning more about myself at this new level of life as I work to serve others.

In the past seven years, I've had the best times, the worst times, the proudest, most meaningful, and purposeful times of my life.

I wouldn't change the good or bad luck for anything, knowing what I know now: Everything was strategically orchestrated by the hands of God to mold me into who I am today. I am beyond blessed to say I'm here, and I choose to be great because God chose me to be just that–Rema the Great!

After the Tears

SHARONA PRINCE

February 17, 1988, was the worst day of my life. Shawn and I had a huge fight the night before. My grandmother had given him a big, black and white Panda teddy bear that was bigger than him. He wanted to put the bear in the bed with us, but there was no way it would fit in the twin-sized bed we shared. When I refused to let him put the bear in bed with us, Shawn began calling me names, and it turned into an ugly fight.

The next day when I woke up and started getting ready for school, I was coming out of the kitchen, and Shawn walked right past me. Still upset about the night before, I went into our bedroom while Shawn headed to the living room. My mother and his father were asleep in the living room on two separate couches, so Shawn sat in a rocking chair watching cartoons. In the bedroom, I plugged up the iron and heard a pop. The sound wasn't very loud; I looked at the iron, thinking it came from there. But then I heard Shawn scream, "Mommy, it burns!"

I raced to the living room and was horrified to find Shawn with a gunshot wound to his head. I'll never forget my mother's cries as I screamed and woke her up. "Shut the f*** up!" she yelled at me in shock, then scooped Shawn into her arms with tears running down her face. By the time she got him out the door, Shawn was lifeless. The sounds he'd been making stopped.

My grandmother, Big Mama, was a mighty prayer warrior who lived in our building on the same floor as us. My mother ran to her apartment and banged on the door. Big Mama was getting ready for work, and her face dropped when she opened the door and saw the gruesome scene. (Not even a week ago, Big Mama told my mother to clean her house because she'd seen a lot of blood). My mother laid Shawn on the sofa, and Big Mama immediately began praying. A couple of minutes later, Shawn gurgled and was breathing again. The police arrived and instructed Big Mama to get a blanket to wrap Shawn in. The officer grabbed Shawn and fled down six flights of stairs, leaving the rest of us frantic and in shock.

News of the tragedy spread through the family quickly. It was early in the morning, and the rest of the kids walked to school like any other day—everyone except for me. I didn't know what to do with myself as all types of thoughts raced through my head. I kept blaming myself. Maybe I should've told Shawn to go wash his face and brush his teeth, but because of our fight, we weren't speaking. My cousins, uncles, and aunts all ended up in Big Mama's living room praying, crying, and asking questions no one really had the answers to.

My mother went to the hospital, and I tried to go back home, but the police had the apartment taped off with yellow tape, and no one was allowed inside. During the investigation, everyone lingered around, consoling one another. My mother called to tell us Shawn was in ICU, breathing with a monitor. The police came to Big Mama's house to interview me. They took me to our apartment, with my uncle and two of my cousins accompanying me. They asked me about Shawn's father's whereabouts, but I was clueless because when I ran out of the house behind my mother, he was still there. Whose gun was it, the police wanted to know. Who lived in the apartment, and why was one of the bedroom doors locked?

Once they finished questioning me, the officers placed a phone call, and I was told my mother said to look for a beige make-up case. I searched all over for it but couldn't find it anywhere. Something told me to look in my bedroom closet—the "clubhouse" where Shawn and I often played. This particular time, the closet was a mess. I was digging and tossing stuff from side to side when suddenly, I stumbled across a big boot but didn't think anything of it.

I tried moving the boot, but it wouldn't budge. When I looked closer, I spotted Shawn's father, Randy. He put his fingers to his lips, silently instructing me to be quiet. I was so startled, I jumped and backed away from the closet. The police asked what was wrong; when I remained silent, they walked to the closet and found Randy hiding there. They commanded him to get up, manhandling him and yanking on his clothes. Randy was like a father to me—seeing him treated so badly hurt. After a brief scuffle, he was placed in handcuffs and told to put his other shoe on. Unfortunately, he couldn't, so he asked me to do it for him. As I went to help him, the police officer yelled, "No, don't do sh*t for him," as Randy struggled to slide his boot on.

Randy was placed into custody, and I was taken to the precinct without my mother's consent. While there, officers put me in a room and handed me a couple of huge photo albums. They told me to take my time as I looked through them; I was to point out anyone who looked familiar. Unsure of what this had to do with my brother and if he was okay, my heart was heavy, and I struggled not to break down and cry. I tried my best to be brave and cooperate so I could get out of there and go home.

A few minutes later, an officer entered the room, asking if I recognized anyone. Although I recognized a few of them, I shook my head no. The officer stormed out of the room, leaving the door open. I spotted Randy in a holding cell across the hall. I was so happy to see him. He asked me was I okay, and I assured him I was. We communicated until he saw the officer approaching again. The officer asked me a series of the same questions, then left the room again. Randy told me he loved me, and I told him I loved him as well. I began thinking of Shawn, and tears rushed down my face. I just wanted my mother and to go home. The officer came back and told me he was taking me home. As I stood and walked past Randy, my heart hurt to tell Randy goodbye.

Several family members were waiting at the apartment when I got there. Everyone asked what happened at the precinct, but I was more concerned about my mother and Shawn, who were still at the hospital. The news my family delivered was devastating: if Shawn lived, he would be a vegetable. I didn't have enough time to come to grips with the diagnosis before we received the phone call that destroyed my life. Shawn was dead.

My tenth birthday was a couple of days before Shawn died at age five. He found a gun in the apartment and accidentally shot himself in the front of his head; the bullet came out the back. I was born and raised in a Pentecostal family—our faith in God was all we had. When Shawn died, I was so angry with God. I couldn't understand how He didn't answer our prayers. Why would He take my little brother? All I could ask was WHY? Why God? It was so hard for me. I cried nonstop.

News of Shawn's death made the front page of the local newspaper. Everyone was aware of the incident, and many people reached out to offer condolences and such. Shawn was in kindergarten and was in love with his teacher Ms. Butler, who reached out to say the class bulletin board was filled with twenty-three hearts representing the students for Valentine's Day, but one heart was missing. When she looked on the floor, she noticed it was Shawn's. His heartbroken classmates made cards that were given to my mother. This was a tragic incident I wasn't sure I'd ever recover from.

Later that day, the Bureau of Child Welfare (B.C.W.) visited our home. The social worker happened to be a good friend of my mother, so we thought everything would be fine. But unfortunately, I was removed from my mother's care because a child had gotten ahold of a gun. I'd just lost my brother; now I was losing my mother too. Life was so unfair and cruel. It was too much to bear.

I needed my mother, and she needed me. My life had changed in a blink of an eye.

The social worker asked if a family member was willing to take custody of me. My mother assured them Big Mama would without a doubt. Big Mama took me in, and I was content knowing I'd be with my favorite person in the world. If there was such a thing as perfect, she was it in my eyes and the eyes of others as well. People called Big Mama a prayer warrior, often saying she had visions that would come to pass. Big Mama called me her prayer partner because she came home with a headache one day, and since I hated seeing her in pain, I prayed. I prayed for Big Mama's headache to go away, and ten minutes later, my prayer was answered. Big Mama started crying and praising God. I felt my own power in that moment.

Living with Big Mama had many perks. The best of them all was that I was allowed to see my mother on a daily basis. This made life more bearable, but life was still hard. I wanted to return home with my mother. I wanted my brother back. Unfortunately, we don't always get what we want.

Shawn's funeral was held on February 22, 1988, in Brooklyn at the Matthew Barret Funeral Home. I dreaded for that day to come. I was so broken, bitter, heartbroken, and nervous that I cried endlessly as I sat on the front row staring at my baby brother's lifeless body lying in the tiniest casket I'd ever seen. He was dressed in a white suit with a red shirt, his hands were folded, and his face was swollen. Next to him was a teddy bear and a plaque that read: **Shawn Prince**. Our family was hit hard by Shawn's unexpected death. All my aunts, uncles, cousins, neighbors, teachers, the school principal, and friends packed the funeral home. I stared at my brother until my eyes filled with tears and more tears. I cried so much, I made myself sick.

After the funeral, everyone gathered at our house for the repast. People were talking and laughing like nothing ever happened, but I was distraught and wanted to be left alone. I went into my mother's bedroom and began separating Shawn's pictures from others. "Why," I cried as I stared at the photos, reminiscing about our short time with each other. Shawn and I fought like cats and dogs, but no one else could mess with us. We had each other's back to the fullest. I was so greedy, I pretended to be his dog to get him to feed me his food. I'd get on my knees, barking and begging until he fed me all of it. Once the food was gone, I told him I didn't want to be a dog anymore, and he never caught on.

The next day was Shawn's burial at Fredrick Douglass Cemetery on Staten Island. My poor mother was a wreck. She couldn't believe her baby was really gone. I could only imagine what was going through her mind. I didn't have to wonder what Big Mama was thinking because she kept screaming, "I'm coming to join you, Shawn!" I hated seeing them like that, but I was praying this was all a bad dream we could wake up from. Unfortunately, it wasn't. It was my reality, and I had no clue how I was going to cope with it.

The days following Shawn's death were miserable. I started collecting quarters made in 1982 because that was his birth year; I put them in his sheepskin coat in remembrance of him. I stared at his pictures and cried myself to sleep. Just when I thought I couldn't take anymore, it was time for me to go back to school.

My friends and teachers were happy to see me, but I was grieving badly and didn't want to be bothered. I just wanted to be left alone.

But life wouldn't leave me alone. A month later, my grandfather was shot in the neck at a gas station. Authorities believed my grandfather was the intended target, but he wasn't. Fortunately, he survived, but now my grandmother's home was no longer safe for me either. First my brother, then my mother—now, I lost Big Mama, too. My world was shattered into a million pieces. I didn't know how to cope but, I knew I had to be strong. I was all I had.

Once my school learned about the incident, my fourth-grade teacher, Ms. Johnson, stepped up to the plate and opened her door to me. I was too numb to even know how to feel. Ms. Johnson had a beautiful corner house in Brooklyn, where I had my own room. It was spacious, and I even had a computer. It didn't matter what I had, though; I was miserable and couldn't stop crying. I wanted my family more than anything.

Our first car ride to school was agonizing, but thankfully Ms. Johnson was reading my mind. I was so embarrassed to be living with my teacher and didn't want my peers to find out, so she let me out on the corner, and I walked the rest of the way. This arrangement worked for a while until one of my classmates spotted me getting out of her car one day. Almost instantly, I was the talk of the school. I was humiliated! It was too much for a ten-year-old to deal with. Ms. Johnson was such a loving and caring person and treated me so kind. I was thankful to be with someone familiar, but I desperately wanted my mother. I missed my family and needed them badly. Ms. Johnson could tell I was unhappy and tried helping in every way possible. It was nothing personal towards her; I just wanted to go home. I wanted my mommy!

Two months passed by, and I was removed from Ms. Johnson's home. I was placed with my aunt on my father's side, who lived in Flatbush, Brooklyn. She had two children around my age. Although I was familiar with them, I didn't want to go there, either. Living with my aunt, I got to see my grandparents, my little sister, and my cousins on my father's side more. My grandparents lived in East New York, Brooklyn, and I visited them often. Sometimes, it was awful having to go there because my sister and I got into fights where she'd say, "That's why your brother's going to hell for killing himself!" That was the meanest thing I'd ever heard, but when I told my mother about it, she told me to shrug it off because my sister didn't know any better.

My aunt took good care of me, making sure I was treated like everyone else, especially on birthdays and holidays. But one day, while visiting my mother, I told her I didn't want to go back. After making a few phone calls, she told me I didn't have to. My uncle Doc took me back to Brooklyn to retrieve my belongings, but unfortunately, my cousin was instructed not to open the door for anyone. Everything Big Mama had given me was in there, and I snapped. On both sides of the door, my cousin and I argued, but she acted like I was a stranger and refused to open the door. I was livid, but she didn't budge.

Following that incident, Shawn's grandmother volunteered to take me in her custody in Crown Heights, Brooklyn, but reconsidered because her house was filled with boys. Deciding it would make better sense for me to stay with her daughter, who had three girls and lived a couple of blocks away, so I ended up there. I'd practically grown up with the girls and was comfortable with them. Finally, this was the closest I'd felt at home since being removed from my own home and Big Mama's. It was almost a year after Shawn's death, and I was still mourning, but at least now there were good days. My first summer there was like none other. I met new people and made lots of friends. Sterling Place turned into my safe haven.

Everything was going great until February 5, 1989. That's when my mother called and dropped the news I dreaded most: Big Mama had died. Life after the passing of my brother and grandmother was detrimental to my health. I spent so many sleepless nights crying and begging God to tell me why He'd taken them from me. I suppressed my feelings and slipped into a deep depression. When I was alone, all I did was cry. Life changed for the worst overnight. I was homesick, and all the crying made it worse. Big Mama taught me that we are never to question God, but I was filled with questions.

My grandmother was a God-fearing woman, mother of the church, and never cursed, drank, or smoked. She went to church three times a week. If there were such a thing as perfect, it would have been Big Mama. It took me seven years to be able to talk about hers and Shawn's deaths without bursting into tears. I was so hurt behind losing them.

When I moved to Sterling, I met a boy named Eric; I was ten, and he was twelve. Eric became my outlet, my go-to person. He asked me out one day, and we became boyfriend and girlfriend shortly after. Eric was so attentive; talking to him was like having my own personal diary. I opened up to him about all the pain I'd endured, and he never judged me. Although we were young, we fell in love.

Eric made sure I was good at all times. He bought me jewelry, teddy bears, toiletries, etc. Even though my aunt told me I was too young to be in love, Eric and I started planning a future together. Through the pain, God placed Eric in my life, and he was my sunshine after the storm.

Planning my future eased the pain. Eric and I were in synch with one another. Regardless of what happened or what I endured, he always made me smile; he made it impossible to stay upset with him for very long. We dated for four years without being intimate. He worked at a tire shop and was a great provider at a young age. He taught me how to love and showed me how I should be treated by men.

By the third year of our relationship, I realized although my losses tore me apart, God put someone in my life to help repair my broken heart. We had a special connection. I remember my grandmother would say, what doesn't kill you makes you stronger; I was getting stronger every day. My motto for my life is, "If I can get through the deaths of my brother and grandmother, I can get through anything!"

I've seen how God works in mysterious ways and how there is always light at the end of the tunnel. He's amazing! I ended up living in a group home and never returned to my mother. Everything happens for a reason, even when we don't understand. Situations can mold us and be used as a stepping stool. I encourage you to grow through what you go through. God knows best, and

He makes no mistakes. I survived what I thought would kill me… there's strength after the tears!

The Battle

SHERYL MASON

In July 2015, I went in for a routine mammogram. Due to my family's medical history of having breast cancer, I've been getting tested since the age of 25, so I didn't think much of it, especially when the initial results were "normal." But then September 23rd, I had a follow-up appointment with the doctor. Additional tests were run—a mammogram, sonogram, and biopsy on my breast and lymph nodes. I sat there going through the motions as the doctors were awestruck by how I watched every step in the process, even the graphic biopsy. To them, I was strong and brave. To me, there was nothing to fear; this was common for me. As it turned out, after four long hours, nothing was common any longer. I was diagnosed with breast cancer.

Hearing the diagnosis rocked me. Had I heard correctly? There's no way the results could be right, so I requested a second opinion and was given the number of a cancer specialist. As soon as I left the hospital, I scheduled an appointment that would be in three days. Until then, I blocked out my concerns and resumed my daily activities.

When the day came for my appointment with the specialist, he asked why I wanted a second opinion. "I don't believe the diagnosis," I said. I went on to share with him how in her 40s, my mother was diagnosed with breast cancer. She fasted 40 days and 40 nights and was healed following the fast. The doctors were amazed and couldn't make sense of what happened, but Mama could—she told them that God did it. After sharing Mama's testimony, the doctor exclaimed that I was crazy, prompting me to leave his office in anger. He made me feel worse than I did when I came through the door. I wished I'd never gone there.

After that dreadful visit, I returned to the initial doctor's office and met with a breast cancer surgeon and her partner, a cosmetic surgeon. Speaking to them gave me hope. They discussed my options and promised to do their best to restore me back to myself and reconstruct my breast after surgery. Feeling like I was in good hands, I made the decision to go through with the surgery they suggested.

On October 7, 2015, a mastectomy was performed on my right breast. I was blessed to have my family there to support me. After four grueling hours, the surgery was a success. As relieved as I was, reality sank in once I returned home. Several times a day, I had to drain fluid from my breasts. It was so painful; I often cried during the process. I also had to change my wrap in order to keep my breasts clean to avoid infection, which was excruciating. For more than six weeks, I could not sleep on my stomach, which is my favorite position, so I barely slept. I had constant headaches and was miserable.

It wasn't long before hopelessness, emotional turmoil, and loneliness crept in. How would the surgery affect my marriage? My husband and I had been through many things before, but breast cancer was a first, and I felt disfigured. I was emotional, and the solitude gave me plenty of time to think, even if it was irrational. Many days, I wondered if I was being punished for my wrongdoings. On top of beating myself up, I felt like I didn't have a support system. It was mine and God's fight alone.

During a follow-up visit with my surgeon, we discussed my mental health, agreeing it would be best for me to get one-on-one counseling. I found a female therapist at a clinic near my home who encouraged me to open up and talk about my feelings and experience. She also urged me to resume my everyday life: cooking, shopping, and helping others. After six months of visits, we agreed to terminate services because of the progress I'd made. I did as the therapist advised and returned to my normal routines. Life was good until July of 2018…when I was diagnosed with breast cancer for the second time.

Weeks prior to the diagnosis, I felt weird, so I discussed my concerns with my surgeon. She sent me for testing and found the cancer had returned in the lymph nodes of my right arm. She suggested I go for chemotherapy, which only ticked me off because I didn't want to do chemo. In the flesh, I was done with all of the treatments, but I heard God say He would never leave nor forsake me. He promised to be with me all the days of my life.

Four days later, I began chemotherapy. I went once every twenty-five days, for a total of eleven sessions. Going to the sessions from 7:30 a.m. to 4:30 p.m. felt like a full-time job. I was medicated intravenously through my hand, which in itself was an answered prayer because that meant I wouldn't have a port inserted into my chest. God also granted my request for a private room, where I prayed and read my Bible during sessions. I had time to think about my family, who initially wasn't aware that I was undergoing chemo. *What if I never returned home? What would they think? How would they feel? These overwhelming thoughts eventually led me to reveal my secret; the burden was lifted, but the fight remained.*

Chemo left me worn down and tired. I was weak and barely ate because the treatments destroyed my taste buds. So, I was given steroids, which produced a ravaging appetite. Chemo had other nasty side effects, too. After my first treatment, my stomach was bloated as big as a balloon for four days. My face, hands, and feet were discolored; my toenails came off, which is the most bizarre thing I've ever seen. I was preparing to bathe one day and couldn't believe my eyes when I looked down and saw my feet. I put my glasses on and saw that my toenails were gone. I was so scared, I wanted to run from my own feet. Needless to say, chemo drains the life from your body, and sucker punches you, leaving you lifeless.

Following chemo came radiation. Treatments were five days a week, in fifteen-minute increments for five months. I hated it! As soon as I got out of the car, I'd begin feeling anxious. Simply seeing the building made me hyperventilate. One day, I panicked so badly, I wound up in the emergency room. Radiation also destroyed my skin. It was hard, like I'd imagine a corpse would be. Surprisingly I didn't dry out. My doctors were astonished at how my skin maintained its moisture and elasticity. I was so happy when I was finally finished with radiation.

Following treatment, I scheduled visits with the oncologist four times a year and once a year with my surgeon. My follow-up appointments went well; in 2019, the cancer was in remission, and my doctors were pleased with my progress. The oncologist advised me to watch my diet and exercise, then prescribed Anastrozole, a medication to decrease estrogen levels and reduce cancer cell growth. Two years later, I still take it daily, deeming it my "life-saving pill."

Breast cancer tried to kill me and snuff me out, but it strengthened me and made me better. It gave me a new lease and perspective on life. Through my battle, God has been with me, providing me with something bigger and better on the other side of turmoil. On the days when I didn't want to get up, God pulled me out of despair. It felt like a force bouncing me out of bed—similar to a trampoline. Any time I felt down and weak, God made me get up. I'm so grateful He didn't let me quit. I want to inspire and encourage other women on their journey. I want them to know they can put their hope, faith, and trust in God because He's able.

Daddy Issues

SHERYL NICOLE

The first man whose duty it was to protect my heart broke it. His poor choices left me fatherless and without a good example of how a man should love a woman. His recklessness stripped me of my foundation, and I foolishly searched for love in men who didn't have the capacity to fill or even feel the void I experienced. I grew up feeling emotionally abandoned. But as I've evolved, I realize God's unconditional love for me and the love I have for myself is more than enough. His love rises above all and has given me the solid foundation on which I now stand firmly planted in my purpose.

At 17-years-old, my father was a mere baby himself when I came roaring into his world. But even on the cusp of manhood, my mother says he did what was necessary to make sure his baby girl had everything she needed. It's too bad he couldn't see what I needed most was his presence. See, for more than half of my life, my father was incarcerated. I was two years old when he first went to prison. He was briefly released for a few months when I was a pre-teen; however, he quickly got caught up in the same lifestyle that landed him locked up in the first place. Consequently, he was forced to serve the rest of his sentence, robbing me once again of the opportunity to be fathered. Equally as devastating was that his promise to rescue my brother and me from the foster care system disappeared right along with him. Abandoned yet again, I was brokenhearted.

Growing up without my father was rough. What was even worse was knowing of him, yet not knowing him past the man in prison whose face was identical to mine. Our DNA was more attached than we were. The man my mother often took me upstate to visit as a little girl was virtually a stranger. Why did I have to go see him in *that place*? I hated those jailhouse visits! Seeing the man I so desperately wanted to be on the outside to take me on daddy-daughter dates and teach me about life, caged in with restricted movements while under the hawking eyes of the guards, sent me into hysterics during our visits. Hiding my face in my hands, I willed myself to become invisible as I cried my eyes out. Daddy tried his best to comfort me, but I was inconsolable. At three years old, I decided that I didn't want to go back to *that place* and told my mother so. Thankfully, she granted my wish and allowed me to stay with family when she visited Daddy.

Over the years, my father called and sent pictures, birthday cards, and letters in an attempt to forge a relationship with me. He never failed to tell me how much he loved and missed me, and promised to make up for lost time once he came home. In my young mind, once we were reunited, he'd be the "best" father, and we'd have the "perfect" relationship. I loved him and eagerly awaited the day he'd come home to begin our "perfect" life together.

In the meantime, Daddy's baby girl was morphing into a teenager. Puberty hit, and it wasn't long before my breasts garnered the attention of pubescent boys. Initially, I wasn't interested in them because I figured they were only after sex. To me, other girls my age were "stupid" and "naïve" to think these little boys liked them, when all they really wanted was access to their bodies. That's why I shocked myself when I transformed into the same stupid, naïve girl I judged them to be.

I don't remember exactly how I met Dennis, but I was 15, and we instantly hit it off. Before long, we were boyfriend and girlfriend. At 19, Dennis was just the mature man I needed. What I liked about him most was that he didn't pressure me for sex, because I wasn't interested in it, anyway. I had a front-row seat to my friends' heartbreak at the hands of boys who'd done them dirty after they slept together and vowed not to make that same mistake—a vow I ended up having no control of keeping.

Dennis and I spent as much time together as possible. I faithfully stopped by his house on my way to and from school every single day. One of our favorite things to do was kiss and make out, but we never went all the way. One evening, I got caught up and stayed at his house past my curfew. I hurried home, only to be turned away by my foster mother, who coldly told me to go back and stay wherever I'd come from. Dejected, I retreated to Dennis's house. He lived with his older male cousin, who'd grown accustomed to seeing me around, so I was welcome to stay the night, but he warned us my overnight stay wasn't to become a regular occurrence.

As we lay down to go to sleep, Dennis started kissing and caressing me. I knew that night would be the night. Foreplay led to the inevitable, but Dennis struggled to break my hymen. Growing frustrated, he blatantly told me I'd have to let someone else do it. The still, dark room swallowed my utter disbelief. We both went silent and eventually drifted off to sleep.

The next morning, my immature, vain teenage self couldn't fathom being caught dead in yesterday's outfit, so I skipped school. We grabbed breakfast from the corner store, and then I went with him to run some errands. When we got back to Dennis's place, we made out as usual. He told me he wanted me, but didn't want to hurt me, then repeated what he said the night before. I was perplexed; *how could my boyfriend want another man to take my virginity?* Sensing my dismay, Dennis worked up the courage to try again and was successful. It hurt badly, but the pain I felt wouldn't compare to the pain I'd soon experience.

Sex is overrated, nothing like what I'd seen in the movies. It's especially awful when you're a terrified virgin. Nevertheless, after we did it the first time, Dennis and I were intimate another three times. It never got better, not even a little bit. I didn't enjoy it, I simply did it to make him happy. I was in love, smitten, or whatever my immaturity tried to justify it as. Whatever I called it, I eventually found out it was anything but love.

One day, Dennis informed me he was going out of town for a few days to do a moving job with his uncle. Of course, I wasn't happy being apart from him, but I had no idea the brief separation would be permanent. The day he was supposed to return home, Dennis left a note for me with his cousin letting me know that although he popped back in town quickly, he was getting back on the road to help his uncle with another job. He said he missed me and would see me soon. That was the last time I heard from him.

I was crushed and heartbroken. Trying to make sense of it all, I couldn't think, eat, or sleep. *Why had Dennis abandoned me after we shared something so special? Didn't I mean anything to him?* For weeks, probably months, I stopped by his house every day to see if he'd finally returned so I could get answers to my questions. Each time I learned that he wasn't there, my heart shattered into even smaller pieces.

Patience worn thin, Dennis's cousin blatantly told me I was wasting my time because he wasn't coming back. He didn't even bother sparing my feelings, claiming he warned me about getting mixed up with Dennis in the first place. I don't remember him ever saying anything like that, but I do recall his cold, indifferent attitude toward me that day. I was humiliated. *How could I give up my precious virginity to a man who left me as if it meant nothing?* I never recovered from Daddy leaving me; now, my broken spirit had to suffer at the hands of another unavailable man.

I worked on mending my broken heart as best as my young, teenage self knew how. I had never experienced this type of heartbreak, so I didn't know how to navigate it. Initially, I withdrew from the world, especially boys. Just my luck, they still wanted me—even more when I rejected them. Before long, loneliness and wanting to feel loved entangled me in a web of promiscuity. I was looking for love where there was none to be found. It was a vicious cycle: a boy expressed interest in me, began his pursuit, and chased until I was entangled in his web. In return, I opened my heart to him, surrendered my body, and latched onto him emotionally. Getting what he wanted, the boy lost interest, leaving me feeling used, discarded, and heartbroken.

I recognized the pattern and knew better, but I didn't do better. Each time, I simplemindedly thought having sex would have a different outcome. "He'll stick around if I give more of myself to him," I foolishly convinced myself. As I got older, my naivety became, "He'll choose me if he sees how good of a woman I am," or "If I do XYZ for him, he'll see my worth."

Absolutely none of that mattered because I hadn't chosen myself. I devalued the woman I was. Consequently, for years, I ran through the gamut of unavailable men. There was the cutter who self-mutilated for attention and abused his ex-girlfriend. He once put his hands on me, too. Then there was the narcissistic professor–10 years my senior, who was sleeping with one of his students. He had the audacity to tell me to my face that he was in a relationship with me, but "f*cked young b*tches." Let's not forget the "actor" who gave an Oscar-worthy performance when he asked for my hand in marriage after our first sexual encounter, only to ghost me months later with no explanation. Or the self-proclaimed *King*, who publicly revered Black women as "God." But that title only pertained to slimmer women because I was "bigger than what he was attracted to" and "wasn't what he wanted." Yet, he was overweight and out of shape himself.

Oh, what about the homeless companion I had who laid up with me in the Airbnbs I rented, but didn't view homeless me as marriage material because I was "like a teddy bear on the curb." According to him, men wanted the teddy bear behind the glass case. Of all the Mr. Wrongs I went through, my ex-husband wins the prize for the best of the worst. Why? Turns out he only married me for citizenship, and threatened to take half of everything when we divorced.

Each failed relationship took a harsh toll on me. My fragile heart was close to shattering beyond repair. Why was this happening to me over and over again? Maybe I had daddy issues after all. Had my father been around to set the example for how a man ought to love, respect, and treat a woman, I probably wouldn't have gone through so much unnecessary heartache.

I began thinking perhaps I'd never find true love or have the family I strongly desired. I was hurting and hopeless; my quest for love threatened to destroy me, but thank God for comforting the brokenhearted. Each time my heart took another hit, God wrapped me in His loving arms, mended my heart, and renewed my mind. He reminded me of His unconditional love for me and His promise to give me my heart's desires. It was my relationship with Him that needed work in order for me to be in happy, healthy relationships with others. I needed to trust and seek Him. I also needed to forgive myself, my father, and the men who hurt me.

My journey to healing began by seeking God first. The power of His Word, prayer, fasting and fellowship gave me the strength I needed. He taught me to repent and forgive. To be forgiven, I had to forgive myself and others, and ask for forgiveness from those I'd wronged, too.

Working on forgiveness forced me to look closely at the whole picture. Including the fact that oftentimes, I didn't make the best choices when it came to dating and relationships. While my father was absent for most of my life, he was not the blame for my mistakes. Of course, having him present would have taught me what it means to be loved by a man, but I hold myself accountable for my poor decisions, especially when I knew better. Furthermore, I was the common denominator in all of my relationships; my lack of self-love was the real root of the problem.

My therapist also helped me realize that my relationship problems didn't originate with my father, but stemmed from lacking an intimate relationship with my Heavenly Father. I didn't trust God to give me the desires of my heart, so I took matters into my own hands. Out of desperation to be a wife and mother, I often settled for less than I deserved. I had to forgive myself for not valuing and loving myself enough to require more from the men I dealt with; I had to forgive them, whether the pain they caused was intentional or not. Forgiveness set me free and helped me escape bitterness. Being bitter robs us of peace and joy—I chose to be better.

By no means is my life perfect, nor do I have everything all figured out. Healing and forgiveness is an ongoing process that I choose every day because I know my restoration isn't just about me. God has chosen me to help others navigate the process of transitioning from hurting to healing. It's my purpose. It's my calling. It's my passion, and God has given me preparation, permission, and provision. Thank you, *Daddy*, for choosing me.

Fire Starter

SIMONE S. GRAY

When I was in second grade, I went from being labeled the sweet, lovable little girl whom my family adored, to a detestable, problematic child. This is what my seven-year-old self believed for years.

It all started with a movie that turned my reality into drama. The day my mother brought home *Playing with Fire*, starring one of my favorite childhood stars, Gary Coleman, is forever etched in my mind. I was immediately intrigued and couldn't wait to watch it. As a parent of two, I now realize my mother had good intentions when she put my little sister and me in front of the television to watch that movie. I believe she thought we'd see the dangers of fire and playing with matches. She could never have imagined the destructive outcome of me watching that film.

Well, the movie did the job Mom intended for my sister, but for me, it had the opposite effect. It imparted something extremely dangerous inside me and provoked my obsession with fire and matches. Any chance I got to strike a match, I did. I waited until everyone was either asleep or distracted and lighted the stove just to see the fire and flames. I was entranced during my time alone with fire. Thinking back on it now, the spirit of self-destruction was unleashed in my life and was doing its best to take me out.

One day after school, like so many times before, I was in the bedroom, bored and unattended. My father was at work, my mother was on the phone, and my little sister was in the living room watching television. With nothing else to do, the urge to strike a match overcame me once again. I struck a match, then another. At first, I thought nothing of it...but then the whole book of matches caught on fire!

Panicking, I hastily tossed the book of matches onto the dresser; the flames seemed gigantic to me. "Put the fire out, Simone!" I told myself. I quickly looked around, hoping to find something to put out the flames, when I spotted a bottle of nail polish remover. To a seven-year-old child, water and nail polish remover looks the same, so they must have the same effects, right? Employing my adolescent logic, I opened the bottle and poured the solution directly onto the flames. What happened after that was a complete miracle.

Rather than engulfing me in flames, the fire jumped from the dresser over my head and landed on my mother's brand-new silk comforter, which was completely flammable. I was in the middle of a burning dresser and a burning queen size bed, unharmed. God divinely protected me.

Within seconds, that little matchbook fire grew into a wildfire! Everything was in flames: the dresser, my parents' bed, the ceiling.

Everything was burning, except me. I was frozen in the middle of the thick black smoke, trying to think of what to do to make everything right. I ran to the bathroom and filled a pail with water to put out the fire, but that made it worse. Finally, my mother ran into the bedroom with a look of utter shock and confusion etched on her face. "Simone, what did you do?" she yelled.

I bolted from the house in my undergarments, raced down the block to the fire station around the corner from us, and frantically ran up to one of the firemen. "Please help me; our home is on fire!" I cried. What followed is still a blur. Soon after the firemen put the fire out, one of them asked if I was okay. I was shaken, but thank God no one had been injured. The fireman got on one knee, held my hand, and asked me in a caring voice, "Simone, what happened?"

I looked him in his bright, blue eyes and confessed I'd been playing with matches. When my mother overheard my admission, the look in her eyes burned worse than the flames. "How could you do this, Simone? Why would you do this to Mommy?" She questioned like I was a stranger. "Get her away from me now!" She gave the firemen my father's number and instructed them to call and have him come get me. When Daddy arrived on the scene, he asked the same question as Mommy.

As remorseful as I was, I didn't have an answer. None of it made sense. Everything happened so fast. I didn't know why I'd done it. Our home was destroyed, almost everything was gone, and I felt horrible. Seeing my mother hurting because of my recklessness nearly ruined me; I hated myself. For years, the devil played with my mind, and I believe it all started from that incident.

He told me I was a horrible person, and no one would ever love me or want me. He said my mother hated me and would never forgive me. And I believed his lies.

We were homeless because of me. Living out of plastic bags, and it was my fault. Because of me, we went from living in a luxury building to being cramped in a shelter. Eventually, I was bounced around and forced to stay with different family members because no one wanted to deal with me. "Nobody wants me," I told myself. I was the problem child, the topic of family gossip and the tea they all wanted to spill. No one knew what to do with me, but they grudgingly had to deal with me. "Simone, why would you do such a thing?" I was asked over and over again. And over and over again, I had no answer to give them.

Not only did I have to deal with the shame of what I'd done, but it also seemed like no one in the family would forgive me. I overheard my grandmother and aunts on the phone talking about it, and my cousins relentlessly teased me. I usually laughed it off, but I was so wracked with guilt, I hated myself and wished I'd never been born. How could I expect anyone to forgive me when I couldn't forgive myself? I wanted to die.

At one point, I became my own worst enemy. The years went on, but I've never forgotten that day. I used to wish I could go back in time to change everything that happened, but time doesn't care about our mistakes. It wasn't until I received Jesus as my Lord and Savior and invited Him into my life that God sent me a gentle reminder: all things were working for my good, and what the enemy intended for bad, God uses for good and His glory. God kept drilling that in my spirit until I actually believed it.

Even as an adult, there was a point where I was acting out in negative, self-destructive ways. I experienced random flashbacks stemming from my childhood, and all the emotions I'd suppressed came rushing back. "What's going on?" I asked God. He revealed that I was suppressing parts of my past that He wanted to heal and deliver me from. He laid on my heart to seek counsel in conjunction with walking with Him, so I did.

Unbeknownst to me, the counselor I chose had experienced some of the very things I had as a child, which made it easy to share the negative feelings and thoughts I had towards myself. I told him everything about my childhood and past leading up to our encounter, which God divinely set up. He asked direct questions, which helped me release the shame that plagued me over the years. The devil thought he had me, but I gave myself permission to forgive my seven-year-old self.

While I no longer play with fire, I'm technically still a fire starter. Only the fire I use now is fire from Heaven. Recently, I learned God uses fire to sanctify and purify His vessels. I use my testimony to show His goodness and all He has done for me and to ignite the fire in others' destinies. I start fires for The Kingdom of God now. Everything that has happened in my life was because God allowed it. If God allowed it, He has a plan for it to be used for good.

God has healed me from the wounds of my childhood mistakes and the lies the enemy used to whisper in my ears. I am not my past, nor am I the mistakes I've made. The trials, tribulations, and painful situations I've survived were all personal invitations from God to get to know Him better. In life, we will go through things, and when we survive, there is a perfecting process that takes place, which transforms us into the person God intends for us to be.

Mistakes, pain, and hurt are inevitable–our perception and how we process it all determines whether we live a life of hindrance or healing. It's all a matter of choice. I choose to heal. God has healed me in order for me to help others heal. I'm on fire to do the work He's set before me, and I'm going to get it done.

Saved by Grace

TONEKIA WILLIAMS

My truth is pretty intense. I thank God for being at the center of my life and healing me from self-inflicted pain. I was so full of hatred for myself and the people around me–there was a nasty taste in my mouth for family, friends, and people who were genuinely happy with themselves. At times, I felt like I was imprisoned in a body other than my own. How could someone who was seemingly pleasant, well-mannered, and helpful be so ugly inside? I constantly battled toxic thoughts as I struggled to understand the contradiction.

Perhaps I was projecting my negative feelings about myself and my parents onto others. I despised my mother for putting men and her addictions ahead of herself, let alone me. In a weird way, I disliked my grandmother as well because her job was to protect me from her daughter's toxicity. Although she did her job, I perceived it as her keeping me away from my mother. As a result, I gave my grandmother hell. She was performing her duties as my protector, but I didn't appreciate her sacrifice. As an adult, I can finally understand and appreciate all she did to raise me.

For many years, the sight of my father made my skin crawl. I blamed him for the tension I had with the opposite sex. The notion of maintaining healthy relationships with men was foreign to me. Slowly, a disease began manifesting within me and caused me to compromise my value to be accepted by men. I was suffering from a fatherless upbringing.

For years, I struggled with accepting my parents as they were, faults and all. As a young girl, I had enough sense to know they weren't living to their fullest potential. Consequently, I often wished I belonged to another family. Why couldn't my parents be more like the Cosbys or the Winslows? I was the product of two broken and misunderstood people who damaged me. The issues I struggled with always reverted back to my parents. Whether it was low self-esteem, awkwardness, or social anxiety—I had to acknowledge their origins each time I was agitated. At one point, I made my mother my human punching bag, constantly attacking her with my words daily.

Deep down, I wanted my mother to feel the pain her mistakes imposed on my life. I held her accountable for my low self-esteem, social anxiety, and depression. On the outside, I was always clean, polished, and dressed in the latest fashion threads; yet I felt like I was the worst looking person in the room and struggled with self-acceptance. In social settings, I found myself drinking to counteract the self-hate that was holding me captive. For years I dreaded attending intimate events; when I did attend functions, I was drunk. I didn't think I was pretty, smart, or talented enough.

I slept on myself for most of my life, but little did I know, I was more than enough.

I'm transparent about my life because I know millions of people are currently struggling with or healing from the issues God has delivered me from. The person I am today has been healed from trauma. To say the least, I was an emotional wreck engaged in a full-fledged war raging inside of me. Eventually, those things I tried to conceal were slowly revealed. Never again will I knowingly hurt myself by bottling things up and not addressing them head-on. How can we heal if we don't acknowledge what we're hurting from?

My grandmother (may God rest her soul) was the perfect example of a phenomenal woman. She was hard-working, confident, and dedicated to God and her family. She worked until she was 67 years old to provide a good life for her children and grandchildren. She honestly taught me everything I know, which confused me when I made poor decisions that weren't aligned with her teachings.

I recall cutting school one morning in 9th grade. While walking to the house my grandmother shared with me, I started thinking about how disappointed she'd feel if she found out her youngest granddaughter—whom she adored, was going against the values instilled in her. How ungrateful was it of me, but the guilt didn't sink in until it was too late.

I was too focused on the basketball player who was walking with me. My naiveté and inexperience were the perfect match for his handsome face, charm, and popularity. He was the guy who told jokes that weren't funny, but every girl in school laughed hysterically. The attention he gave me in that moment was negatively empowering me. I was just an average nobody any other day, but when I was alone behind closed doors with him, I felt wanted. After a few months of the same routine, I came to a sad awakening: Mr. Handsome was dating half of the girls in my high school; I was another fractured human who was added to his collection. He didn't value me, nor did I value myself.

Devaluing myself followed me through adulthood. I failed to put myself first because I idolized people's opinions of me. God blessed me to be kind, empathetic, and giving; however, I didn't use any wisdom along with my characteristics. No matter who it was, I had no boundaries when it came to pleasing people. I constantly felt the need to overcompensate in order to get people to like me. Sometimes I amuse myself thinking about those past situations.

On one occasion, I went out of my way for a close friend for her birthday, which was nothing new for me. It was a blistering cold day, and I took two trains and a bus to go buy a fancy, overpriced birthday cake I thought she would love. After almost falling on ice several times, getting frost-bitten fingers, and carrying the giant cake on the crowded train, I finally arrived at the exclusive dinner party that I'd planned for weeks. The event was a success, and I was happy that my friend and the guests enjoyed themselves. A few days after the party, my friend dropped the bomb that she didn't even like the cake. "It was okay," were her exact words. Talk about livid! My feelings were hurt; I only had myself to blame. I took a mental note and buried her statement in a special vault that I'd become too familiar with.

Dealing with my family was no different. Though we have the same blood in our veins, I felt like I had to impress them as well, which made me resent some of the people closest to me. Never did I sit down and think, "Tonekia, you're the real problem; go somewhere and love yourself." I blamed others for my shortcomings and tormented myself instead of talking to God about how I felt.

The Bible tells us in Matthew 11:28 to go to God, and He will give us rest. Time and time again, I stood in my own way, ignored the Word, and leaned on my own understanding until I was eventually forced to submit to Him. Honestly, we never know what people are battling. From the age of four, I was hit with attacks and adversity. My life has been like a rollercoaster; however, trauma birthed so many great things in me. You never know what you are capable of until you grow through what you go through and surrender it to God.

I'm glad my transparency can help others–this is OUR journey! My advice to the bruised yet beautiful people reading my testimony: Stop pretending you're healed and allow yourself to heal for real. Yes, a broken crayon can still color; however, a whole crayon is more beneficial. You can comfortably hold it and color with more precision. Forgive yourself and the people who hurt you. Operate in wholeness–you owe it to yourself.

In Genesis 1:27, the Bible says God created us in His own image. Do you know how powerful that is? God is mighty, strong, everlasting, honorable, creative, beautiful, and a pure delight. Therefore, if we are created in the image of greatness, how can we indulge in anything less than the very best version of our whole self? We are fearfully and wonderfully made. Love yourself, as there is only one YOU. Shine bright. Your past does not dictate your present self; don't hold who you were against who you are becoming. You are enough!

I was saved by the grace of God. The pain which resided inside held me hostage from my true potential. Once I laid my burdens at God's feet, my beauty awakened, inside and out. No longer did I bleed on others, I dealt with my problems from the root, beginning with me. Remember, hurt people hurt people. By the grace of God, I walked out of my hurt, so will you.

Repeat after me: *I decree and declare I am healed, I am whole, I am restored, and renewed. My pain had a purpose that was bigger than me. I refuse to bow down to the troubles, adversities, or suffering of the world. I am living proof of the mercy and grace of God. I am a new creation; I will continue to bloom! I have been transformed from hurting to healing. In Jesus Christ's mighty and matchless name, AMEN!!!*

MEET THE AUTHORS

Adrienne Martian

Adrienne is a mother, Certified Public Accountant (CPA), real estate developer, and author. As a first-generation Caribbean-American, Adrienne has dedicated her life to serving others and imparting the importance of building generational wealth. She is the founder of FAME Consulting LLC; providing quality accounting support to individuals and businesses. She also sits on several non-profit boards dedicated to improving disparities for people of color.

Andrea Moses

Andrea Moses is a mother, entrepreneur, and aspiring motivational speaker. She recently underwent a yearlong journey of self-love discovery. During that period, Andrea worked through the adversities of addiction and mental health. Now, with strengthened faith and renewed hope, she wants to bring awareness and support to women and teenagers who may be experiencing similar challenges. Andrea strives to bring hope to the hopeless and inspire them to be the author of their own success stories.

Azizah McEntire

Azizah McEntire is a Licensed Mental Health Counselor, author, and speaker. She lives by her personal motto: *It doesn't matter what was done to you or what you've done, you can rise above it.* Azizah's personal experiences in life have taught her that trials prepare you for your victory. She aims to uplift people so they can be victorious over their circumstances. When Azizah isn't helping people succeed in life, she enjoys spending quality time at home with her family—watching a good movie and enjoying a delicious meal.

Camylle Hill

Camylle Hill is a writer, motivational speaker, and educator born and raised in New Jersey. A mother of two, her love of writing began at a young age, with entertaining her siblings with make believe bedtime stories.

She has dedicated her professional life to working with youth to implement writing as a mechanism for coping with trauma and coaching young adults in their career paths. She is currently attending Montclair State University as an MFA candidate and working on her debut novel. under her pen name, *Karmel Ink.*

Candice Davie

Candice Davie is an editor at *Black Bride* and content manager and founder of the women's wellness site, *Simplistic Chic* (www. simplisticchic.com). When she's not looking at interior design ideas on Pinterest or doing workout videos on YouTube, she's living the mommy and wife life with her husband and son in

Atlanta, GA. Connect with her on social @candicesophia_ and @simplisticchic_.

Chanel Prince

Chanel Prince is a mother, educator, and entrepreneur. At age 18, Chanel became a young mother and experienced many hardships and trials. Her experiences gave birth to her passion for encouraging and helping young mothers struggling with low self-esteem and self-doubt, issues she once faced.

Over the years, life's lessons have helped to shape and mold Chanel into the woman she is today. Each day she aspires to be a better version of herself, especially in her role as a mother. Her children are her greatest gift and inspire her daily to be God's best.

Charelle Butler

Charelle Alesha Butler is an esthetician, cosmetologist, entrepreneur, and author. Although she considers herself a novice writer, Charelle has always used journaling to express her feelings and talk to God. After losing her mother and her newborn son within the span of four months, writing helped Charelle to escape the pain, regain control of her life, and find her voice.

She began to allow God to rebuild her from the inside and opened her heart to healing. Through her testimony, she hopes to touch the lives of women who are silenced by the shame and stigmas associated with depression. Furthermore, she desires to be a beacon of hope for anyone that needs to be reminded that they are not alone and that there is not only victory, but healing to be won after the battle.

Ilene Fernandez

Ilene Fernandez was born and raised in Brooklyn, NY. She is a loving mother of two children. She is also an educator and holds a Bachelor's and Master's degree in psychology. Ilene enjoys listening to music and spending time with her family. She is creative, compassionate, generous, and hard-working. Ilene is well-known for partaking in things that push her to develop and grow. She believes that everyone has a purpose in life, and part of her purpose is to help heal people through her writing.

Janice Colbert

Lovingly known as "Nana," Janice Colbert is a mother, grandmother, and great-grandmother, among a host of other titles. One of her greatest passions is mentoring and advocating for seniors and underprivileged people of all ages. But she especially loves using her wealth of wisdom and experience to help others navigate their healing journey. Janice has been referred to as an "evangelist" by some, but simply praises God for being called to do His work. She is overjoyed to do God's work in this purpose project and prays that everyone who reads this anthology will be blessed as they embark on their healing journey.

Julia Long

Julia Long is a wife, mother, grandmother, and entrepreneur. She is also a minister actively studying to become an assistant pastor.

Her passion for writing began as a teenager and has developed over time. She is an avid journal writer who prides herself on being self-reflective. Julia enjoys revisiting old journal entries to see her growth, many life changes, and accomplishments. She strives to help others see their own potential through her writing.

Laura Dulin

Laura Nesha Dulin is a proud mother of five beautiful children. She is an educator and mentor, and most importantly, she is a conqueror. She has faced many roadblocks which were meant to deter her, but she's never been afraid to go "off the beaten path" to make a new way. After much adversity, she obtained a Bachelor's degree in English from Delaware State University and a Master's degree in Secondary Education from Wilmington University.

She lives in Delaware where she works as a High School English Teacher in an alternative setting where she gets to educate and mentor young teens. She is also a board member of a non-profit organization, *I Am Your Sister, Inc.* Having experienced many traumatic experiences throughout her life, she focuses on helping to uplift other women who have gone through or are going through similar situations.

Lena Degraff

Lena Degraff is a mother, telecommunications technician, and a registered nurse. She was born and raised in Brooklyn, NY.

She's lived in Brooklyn all her life but loves to travel the world. Traveling allows her to learn new cultures and meet new people. Lena plans to visit each state in the United States of America before she reaches the perfectly ripe age of 50.

Monica L. Whiting-Hogans

Monica L. Whiting-Hogans was born and raised in Mount Vernon, NY. She is a graduate of Morgan State University and holds a master's degree in Business from Mercy College. Monica is an accountant by trade, but also has a passion for writing, baking, and mentoring young girls.

She is a proud and active member of Alpha Kappa Alpha Sorority, Incorporated® and sits on the executive board for *Wheeler, Wilson, and Johnson Community Projects, Inc.* and on the Board of Directors for the *Mount Vernon Day Care Center.* She is also a charter member of the *NY Downstate Business and Professional Women's Club of the National Association of Negro Business and Professional Women's Clubs, Incorporated.*

Quanda Dulin

Quanda Dulin was born and raised in New York. After high school, she attended Norfolk State University, where she earned both her Bachelor of Arts in Psychology and Master of Social Work. She has excelled in her field of study and is currently a Licensed Clinical Therapist and Certified Sex Offender Treatment Provider. She is currently employed as the Director of the *Veterans Outreach Center* within the Department of Veterans Affairs and serves on the *Mental Health Council for the Veterans Health Administration.*

Quanda also has a private practice in which she provides individual, family, couples, and marital therapy—specializing in trauma-informed care. She attributes her strong background in psychology and mental health as being essential in her own path to healing. Her greatest accomplishment is lovingly raising her two children Assata and Mekhai.

Shanisha Collins

Shanisha Collins, a native of Northeast Ohio, is an entrepreneur who is passionate and dedicated to providing dynamic experiences as a user experience professional and cleaning business owner.

Shanisha has a keen understanding of how experiences, both good and bad, can have a tremendous impact on a person's mental health. She's on a personal mission to unpack her past traumas and break generational curses for the betterment of her children's future.

She enjoys being actively involved in the community and can be found in women, student, and small business empowerment circles. Shanisha finds daily inspiration in the mantra, "Serve to lead."

Sharema Harvell

Sharema "Rema The Great" Harvell is a Harlem-based author, entertainer, producer, and community leader amongst many other titles. Over the past decade, she has fought with bouts of depression, substance abuse, and addiction–triumphantly emerging on the other side. She utilizes her life story to help others who are dealing with their own trials and trauma.

She is currently a group facilitator for an *Alternative to Incarceration* program in East Harlem. Additionally, she is working towards her Master's in social work and looks forward to a possible role as a member of NYC City Council in the future. Sharema states and wholeheartedly believes, "Our only purpose is to take care of each other. As long as you are working in service of others, with full intentions aligning with your actions, you will always be taken care of abundantly".

Sharona Prince

Sharona Charrisse Prince was born and raised in New York City. As a child, she experienced lasting trauma. She learned how to use her pain as a stepping stool to her purpose.

Sharona is a proud mom to five boys. Despite life's twists and turns, she's managed to overcome adversities in pursuit of providing a better life for her children. In 2020, she obtained her Associate's degree in Business Administration and continues to further her education. She currently works as the lead teacher for the after-school enrichment program through Charlotte-Mecklenburg Schools.

Sheryl Mason

Sheryl Mason is a wife, mother, grandmother, and retired chef.

Throughout her career in the culinary industry, she took great pride in knowing that her food made the hearts and stomachs of many rejoice. Her love for cooking began at the age of five, as she often admired her mother while cooking. Sheryl is well-known for her famous "Mama's Sweet Potato Pies," a recipe she adapted from her mother. Although she will always love cooking, Sheryl has decided to trade in her cookbooks to write books that feed the souls of her readers.

Sheryl Nicole

Sheryl Nicole is an educator, serial entrepreneur, best-selling author, coach, and speaker. Her passion for writing was discovered and developed in elementary school during a period of trauma and adversities. Over the years, writing has served as an outlet for Sheryl to express and free herself. In her darkest moments, writing illuminated her life.

Now, writing to inspire healing and change has become her gift to others. Sheryl also enjoys guiding aspiring authors through the self-publishing process, helping them craft and spread their powerful messages. As the founder of *Noire Publishing House*, Sheryl works tirelessly to amplify Black and brown voices and experiences.

Simone S. Gray

Author of the best-selling book, *"Powerful Prayers & Petitions: A Closer Walk with God"*, Simone S. Gray is a certified Life Purpose Coach who uses biblical principles and life experiences to mentor women around evolving into who God intends for them to be.

She combines professional training and personal experiences to assist women in living a God-filled life. Her desire is to please God by walking in her purpose and helping His children in their walk. Simone wholeheartedly embraces her God-given gifts of creating, cultivating, and connecting people for the advancement of the Kingdom of God. She resides in Brooklyn, New York with her husband and their two children.

Tonekia Williams

"I've made countless mistakes in my life, I'm sure I still have some left in me. However, I'm crazy enough to believe I can help change the world by being humble and keeping God first". Tonekia Williams is a prayer warrior, educator, entrepreneur, philanthropist, and author hailing from Brooklyn, NY. She is certain that all of the pain she has endured during her life has strengthened her to help others. "If God doesn't bring us to and through the wilderness, how can we lead others to the kingdom?" she often asks. Tonekia is currently in the process of writing her memoir to share more of her testimony; while simultaneously working on establishing a non-profit organization to help support children and revive communities.

MEET THE AUTHORS

Made in the USA
Columbia, SC
20 June 2021

40761889R00138